Editor

Eric Migliaccio

Managing Editor

Ina Massler Levin, M.A.

Illustrator

Mark Mason

Cover Artist

Marilyn Goldberg

Art Production Manager

Kevin Barnes

Art Coordinator

Renée Christine Yates

Imaging

James Edward Grace

Rosa C. See

Publisher

Mary D. Smith, M.S. Ed.

Reading & Writing

- ✔ Organizational Patterns
- ✔ Literary Language
- ✔ Fables, Myths, & Fairy Tales
- ✔ Making Predictions
- ✔ Character Development
  ...and more!

Ideal for Substitute Teachers

Author

Jessica M. Dubin Kissel, M. A.

Teacher Created Resources

Teacher Created Resources, Inc.

6421 Industry Way

Westminster, CA 92683

www.teachercreated.com

ISBN-1-4206-8032-3

©*2006 Teacher Created Resources, Inc.*

Made in U.S.A.

Table of Contents

Introduction

The Concept

Every teacher needs and deserves more time. And excellent teachers know that to create excellent lesson plans, it takes time. The lessons in *Ready to Go Lessons, Grade 3* are completed lesson plans written specifically for third-grade language-arts teachers to use throughout the year. They will come in handy for teachers who are short on time, need complete substitute lesson plans, or just want a lesson to incorporate into their units—specifically, a lesson that they did not have to take the time to design!

Each lesson is broken down into a reading and writing component. The reading and writing sections of each lesson were designed to enhance one another, but most of them can be taught separately, as well. Each lesson can be easily altered to match different teaching and learning styles.

An Overview

✔ The lessons provided in this book use clearly-written and simply-designed teaching frameworks that are easy to follow.

✔ Depending on the ability of the students, the length of time it will take to complete the lessons will vary.

✔ Most materials that are needed to complete the lesson are included. (All you need to do is make copies!) Sometimes a roll of tape or a pair of scissors will be required, but such items are clearly listed at the beginning of each lesson.

The Lessons

Using national educational standards as a guide, the lessons in *Ready to Go, Grade 3* highlight specific reading and writing strategies. Also included in each lesson are original reading selections, purpose-for-reading questions, a guide to vocabulary development, specific writing assignments, prewriting ideas, organizational guidance for the students, revision and editing instructions, and simple assessment options.

The Assessments

An evaluation sheet is provided at the end of each unit. Every teacher awards points differently, so suggested weights for each objective are not included.

The "possible points" section is left blank. Before making copies, the teacher should fill in how many points the students can earn for mastering each objective. Then, while grading the students' work, teachers can award the points in the "earned points" section.

Extensions

Each lesson comes with an original reading selection. Each reading selection was written with specific lesson objectives in mind, but there are endless variations on what can be done with the reading material.

Lesson One

Objectives

Reading

✔ To identify a biography

✔ To look for compound words

Writing

✔ To write a biography using a paragraph format

✔ To use a topic sentence

✔ To write in complete sentences

✔ To follow rules of capitalization

Lesson Summary

The students will read a biography about Wilson Bentley, the first person to take a photograph of a single snowflake. Then, students will use specific facts to write a biography about Richard Drew, the inventor of Scotch tape and masking tape.

Materials Needed

✸ copies of the reading assignment (page 8)

✸ copies of the writing assignment (page 9)

✸ a blank sheet of paper; scissors; and tape, if available

Part I: The Reading Connection

A. Develop interest in the topic.

Have the students watch you fold a piece of paper into four squares. Cut or tear segments off of the paper. Open up the folded paper to reveal a snowflake.

B. Encourage students to make predictions about the reading.

Explain to the students that they will be reading a biography about a person called the Snowflake Man. Explain to the students that a biography is written information about someone's life.

1. *Ask:* "Why might someone be called the Snowflake Man?" Encourage reasonable answers.

2. *Ask:* "What types of things might we learn about the Snowflake Man from reading his biography?" When reading the Snowflake Man's biography, we might learn about where he lived, when he lived, or why he is called the Snowflake Man. Encourage students to give similar answers.

Part I: The Reading Connection *(cont.)*

C. Encourage good reading habits.

Remind students that some words look long but are still easy to sound out because they are made up of two little words put together. Explain that these words are called *compound words*. An example of a compound word is *snowflake*. It is made up of the words *snow* and *flake*. Encourage students to see if a difficult word is a compound word when trying to sound it out.

D. Establish a purpose for reading.

Pass out copies of "The Snowflake Man" (page 8) for the students to read. Read aloud the questions that the students should answer as they read the story.

1. Why did Wilson Bentley want to take pictures of snowflakes?

2. What can we learn from Mr. Bentley's pictures?

3. Why is Wilson Bentley called the Snowflake Man?

4. Why is "The Snowflake Man" a biography?

E. Define and extend word meaning.

The word *images* is used in the story, and it might be a new word for some of the students. Tell the students to imagine a snowflake in their minds. Explain that what they are seeing in their minds are images of snowflakes, but the snowflakes are not really here to see. Define the word *images*. Images are pictures of things that are not really here to see.

F. Allow ample time for students to read the selection and reflect upon the assigned questions.

G. Discuss the answers to the reading.

Answers to the questions may vary. However, sample answers are as follows:

1. *Why did Wilson Bentley want to take pictures of snowflakes?* Wilson Bentley thought snowflakes were pretty. He wanted to find a way to save their images before they melted.

2. *What can we learn from Mr. Bentley's pictures?* From Mr. Bentley's pictures, we can learn that no two snowflakes are alike.

Part I: The Reading Connection *(cont.)*

G. Discuss the answers to the reading. *(cont.)*

3. *Why is Wilson Bentley called the Snowflake Man?* Wilson Bentley is called the Snowflake Man because he was the first person to take a picture of a single snowflake.

4. *Why is "The Snowflake Man" a biography?* "The Snowflake Man" is a biography because it gives facts about a person's life.

H. Re-examine an element of the story.

Remind the students that *snowflake* is a compound word that was used often in the story. Have the students search for the other compound word in the story. (The other compound word in the story is *snowfall*.)

Part II: The Writing Connection

A. Develop interest in the topic.

Hold up a roll of tape. *Ask:* "Who invented tape? Why do you think somebody invented it? When do you think it was invented?" Allow students to give accurate or creative answers to these questions.

B. Explain the writing assignment to the students.

Say, "A biography is factual writings about a person's life. Today, we will be writing a short biography about the man who invented masking tape and Scotch tape. I will give each of you a list of information about this man. Your assignment is to use the facts to write his biography in the form of a paragraph."

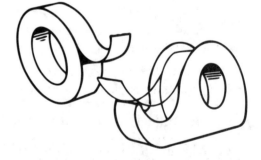

Pass out the information about Richard Drew (page 9). Read aloud the facts for the students.

C. Assist students in organizing their paragraphs.

Remind students that a strong paragraph has a strong first sentence. This sentence is called a *topic sentence*. The topic sentence lets the reader know what the paragraph is going to discuss.

Together with the students, list possible topic sentences on the board. Some examples are the following: Richard Drew is a very important inventor. Richard Drew is a great inventor. Richard Drew's inventions are important to our lives.

Lesson One

Part II: The Writing Connection *(cont.)*

D. Allow writing time.

Give students ample time to write their paragraphs. As they are working, walk around the room offering guidance.

E. Give students a strategy to help them revise their writing.

Point out to the students that the facts on the handout are not written in complete sentences. The students should have put the facts into complete sentences when writing their paragraphs.

Show students an example of a complete and incomplete sentence. For example, "Lived from 1886–1982" might be changed to "Mr. Drew lived from 1886–1982."

Have students check their work to see that they used complete sentences in their paragraphs.

F. Give students a strategy to help them edit their writing.

Review with the students some rules for capitalization. Have students check to see that they have used these rules correctly in their writing. Students should have capitalized:

✴ the first word in each sentence

✴ a person's first and last name

✴ the name of a city or state

✴ brand names of items, such as Scotch tape

G. Publish students' ideas.

Have students write a final draft of their paragraphs. Use Scotch tape or masking tape to attach the paragraphs to the wall.

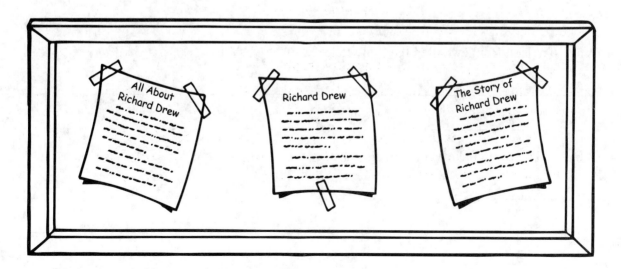

The Reading Assignment

Directions: Read "The Snowflake Man." Use complete sentences to answer the questions below.

The Snowflake Man

Wilson Bentley lived in Vermont, where there was a lot of snowfall. Mr. Bentley thought that snowflakes were very pretty. They reminded him of pieces of art. He wanted to find a way to save the pretty images before they melted.

In 1885, Mr. Bentley took a picture of a single snowflake. He was the first person to do this. He took many pictures of snowflakes after he learned how to do it. These pictures were made into a book. The book is called *Snow Crystals*. We can learn a lot by looking at his book. We can learn that no two snowflakes are alike. Since Wilson Bentley was the first person to take a picture of a single snowflake, he is called the Snowflake Man.

Answer the following questions:

1. Why did Wilson Bentley want to take pictures of snowflakes?

   _____

   _____

2. What can we learn from Mr. Bentley's pictures?

   _____

   _____

3. Why is Wilson Bentley called the Snowflake Man?

   _____

   _____

4. Why is "The Snowflake Man" a biography?

   _____

   _____

Lesson One

The Writing Assignment

Directions: In the form of a paragraph, write a biography about Richard Drew, the man who invented Scotch tape. Use the facts below to help you.

Facts about Richard Drew

* Lived from 1886–1982

* Enjoyed playing the banjo for much of his life

* Lived in St. Paul, Minnesota, during the 1920s

* Noticed that painters were having a hard time painting a straight line on cars

* Invented masking tape to help painters paint in straight lines

* Sold masking tape in stores, and people quickly found many different uses for it

* Invented masking tape in 1923

* Invented Scotch tape in 1930

_____

_____

_____

_____

_____

_____

_____

_____

_____

_____

The Reading Connection

Teacher Direction: Evaluate the answer to reading question number *four*.

Objective	Possible Points	Earned Points
You understand that a biography tells facts about a person's life.		
Total Earned Points:		

The Writing Connection

Teacher Direction: Evaluate the writing assignment.

Objective	Possible Points	Earned Points
You wrote a biography about a person's life.		
You used a topic sentence in your paragraph.		
You wrote your facts in complete sentences.		
You used rules of capitalization.		
You put effort into the writing process.		
Total Earned Points:		

Additional Teacher Comments: _____

_____

_____

_____

_____

Lesson Two

Objectives

Reading

✔ To identify a fairy tale

✔ To read words that end with a silent /e/

Writing

✔ To write a paragraph that could be found in a fairy tale

✔ To use descriptive words

✔ To identify misspelled words

Lesson Summary

The students will read a fairy tale called "The Invisible Castles." Then, the students will write a descriptive paragraph that could be found in a fairy tale.

Materials Needed

✷ copies of the reading assignment (pages 14–15)

✷ copies of the writing assignment (page 16)

✷ dictionaries (*optional*)

Part I: The Reading Connection

A. Develop interest in the topic.

On the board, write the words "COLORS" and "CHOCOLATE." Have the students list as many colors and types of chocolate as they can, and write their suggestions in the appropriate columns.

B. Encourage students to make predictions about the reading.

1. Tell the students that they will be reading a story called "The Invisible Castles." Explain that this story is an example of a fairy tale. Teach students that many fairy tales have castles and royalty (such as kings and guards), evil characters, magic, make-believe creatures (such as dragons), a problem and solution, a lesson, and sayings like "once upon a time" and "happily ever after."

2. Ask students to make predictions about the story. *Ask:* "Based on the title of the story and what you know about fairy tales, what do you think this story might be about?" Allow students to give creative answers.

C. Encourage good reading habits.

Remind students that some words end with the letter *e*, but the ending /e/ sound is silent. For example, the /e/ in *chocolate* in not pronounced. The words *invisible* and *castle* also end with a silent /e/. As students read, they should try to remember that all readers must sometimes sound out words. All readers must remember that the letter *e* is sometimes silent.

Part I: The Reading Connection *(cont.)*

D. Establish a purpose for reading.

Pass out copies of "The Invisible Castles" (page 15) for the students to read. Read aloud the instructions on page 14 for the students.

E. Define and extend word meaning.

The word *replaced* is used in the story, and it might be a new word for some of the students. Tell a student to remove something off of your desk. Return the item to your desk and say, "Now the item is replaced. What does *replaced* mean?" *Replaced* means "put back."

F. Allow ample time for students to read the story and complete the reading assignment.

G. Discuss the solutions to the reading-assignment questions.

Student responses to the following prompts (given on page 14) may vary.

✳ *Circle a description of a castle.* Students might have circled the following description: "Princess Ayala lived in a rainbow castle. Each day, the colors in the castle would change. Nothing was ever the same color twice."

✳ *Draw a crown on top of the name of a royal character.* Students should have drawn a crown on the name of either Princess Yael or Princess Ayala.

✳ *Draw a scary face next to the name of an evil character.* Students should have drawn a scary face next to Dragina's name.

✳ *Draw a magic wand next to a magical event.* Students might have drawn a wand next to the following passage: "One night, Dragina put a spell on the castles. She made each castle invisible to the other."

✳ *Draw a star around a make-believe creature.* Students could have drawn a star around a unicorn or a dragon.

✳ *Put a question mark next to a problem that a character has.* Students might have drawn a question mark next to the sentence "When the princesses woke up, they did not know where their friend had gone."

✳ *Put a checkmark next to a lesson that a character learned.* Students should have put a checkmark next to "As strong as the spell was, the friendship between the princesses was stronger."

Part I: The Reading Connection *(cont.)*

G. Discuss the solutions to the reading-assignment questions. *(cont.)*

✷ *Underline a saying like "once upon a time" or "happily ever after."* Both of these phrases, as well as "a long time ago," can be found in the story.

✷ *Draw a square around a word that ends with a silent /e/.* In the story, *have, made, castle,* and *side* are examples of words that end in a silent /e/.

Part II: The Writing Connection

A. Develop interest in the topic.

List the following on the board: castle, queen, king, princess, an evil character, and make-believe creatures. Have the students select one of these items. Next, have them create images in their minds of the selected items. Once they have done so, have them draw sketches of them.

B. Explain the writing assignment to the students.

Refer to the list of words on the board. Say, "These are all items that can be found in fairy tales. Today, we are going to write a descriptive paragraph about the fairy tale characters or castles that you just drew."

C. Assist students in organizing their descriptive paragraphs.

1. Have the students examine their sketches carefully. Then, encourage students to use their imaginations to make their sketches come alive in their minds.

2. Distribute the student handout (page 16). Help the students gather their ideas. Read aloud the questions on their writing assignment handout and allow them time to answer each question. (Encourage students to be creative, but you might want to let them use the examples provided if they need some ideas.)

3. Have the students start their descriptive paragraphs by writing: "Once upon a time, a long time ago, there was a . . ."

D. Allow writing time.

Give students ample time to write their paragraphs. As they are working, walk around the room and offer guidance.

E. Give students a strategy to help them revise their writing.

Explain to the students that descriptive words are important. They allow someone else to see what they see in their minds. Descriptive words help writers to share their thoughts and ideas.

One way to add descriptive words in writing is to think about the size of the object being described. Have the students reread their paragraphs and add words that describe size—for instance, the length of a character's hair, the size of a creature's wings, the size of a character's crown, or the height of a castle's tower.

Part II: The Writing Connection *(cont.)*

F. Give students a strategy to help them edit their writing.

Remind students that all writers have trouble spelling some words. Have the students reread their paragraphs and underline words that they are not sure how to spell. Have students tell you what some of those words are. Write those correctly-spelled words on the board.

If this exercise begins to take too much time, you can walk around the room while the students are editing and correct their underlined words. Or, you might choose to have students use dictionaries to look up the spelling of a few of their misspelled words.

G. Publish students' ideas.

Place the students' sketches around the room. Read aloud the students' descriptive paragraphs. Have the students match the descriptions with the sketches.

The Reading Assignment

Students Directions: Read the fairy tale "The Invisible Castles" on page 15. As you read, make the following marks on your paper:

- ✱ Circle a description of a castle.
- ✱ Put a crown on top of the name of a royal character.
- ✱ Draw a scary face next to the name of an evil character
- ✱ Draw a magic wand next to a magical event
- ✱ Draw a star around a make-believe creature
- ✱ Put a question mark next to a problem that a character has
- ✱ Put a checkmark next to a lesson that a character learned.
- ✱ Underline a saying like "once upon a time" or "happily ever after"
- ✱ Draw a square around a word that ends with a silent /e/.

The Reading Assignment *(cont.)*

Directions: Read "The Invisible Castles" below.

The Invisible Castles

Once upon a time, a long time ago, there lived two princesses. Princess Ayala lived in a rainbow castle. Each day, the colors in the castle would change. Nothing was ever the same color twice.

The other princess, Princess Yael, lived in a chocolate castle. This princess could eat whatever she wanted. Whatever she ate was replaced with fresh chocolate.

The two princesses were good friends. They liked to play together. They enjoyed eating chocolate and looking at colors together.

There was an evil witch who lived near them. Her name was Dragina. She was jealous of the two friends. Sadly, she did not have any friends at all. One night, Dragina put a spell on the castles. She made each castle invisible to the other.

When the princesses woke up, they did not know where their friend had gone. They each called for their helpers. Their helpers were no help.

Right away, Princess Ayala called for her dragons. She asked them to see what they could find. But Princess Yael's castle was invisible to the dragons, too.

Princess Yael asked her unicorns to find Princess Ayala and her castle. The unicorns' magic could not see through the wicked spell.

Night came. Stars began to glow. Each princess stepped outside at the same time. Each princess looked up at the same star. They each said, "My friend, I hope you are okay." With that, the spell was broken. As strong as the spell was, the friendship between the princesses was stronger.

The princesses lived happily ever after. Since they learned how important friendship was, they asked Dragina if she wanted to be their friend, too. Dragina became a wonderful friend to the princesses. She even used her magic to make a new chocolate for Princess Yael's castle and a new color for Princess Ayala's castle.

Lesson
Two

The Writing Assignment

Directions: Write a descriptive paragraph about a character or a castle that could be found in a fairy tale. Use your answers to the questions below to help you fill in your writing.

Questions to Ask

1. How old is your character or castle?

2. What colors do you see when you imagine your character or castle?

3. What sounds do you hear when you imagine your character or castle?

4. What do you smell when you imagine your character or castle?

5. What textures or materials do you see when you see your character or castle?

6. What is the name of your character or castle?

Once upon a time, there was a _____

_____

_____

_____

_____

The Reading Connection

Teacher Directions: Evaluate the answers to the reading assignment.

Objective	Possible Points	Earned Points
You underlined parts of the story that show that this story is a fairy tale.		
You drew a square around a word that ended with a silent /e/.		
Total Earned Points:		

The Writing Connection

Teacher Direction: Evaluate the descriptive fairy tale paragraphs.

Objective	Possible Points	Earned Points
You began with the words "Once upon a time . . ."		
You used descriptive words to describe your character or castle.		
You put effort into spelling words correctly.		
You put effort into the writing process.		
Total Earned Points:		

Additional Teacher Comments: _____

_____

_____

_____

Lesson Three

Objectives

Reading

✔ To identify a fable

✔ To imagine parts of the story

Writing

✔ To write a mini-fable using a real-life lesson

✔ To use descriptive words

✔ To use commas correctly in descriptions

Lesson Summary

The students will read a fable called "The Secret Teller." Then, students will write a mini-fable using a lesson that they have learned in their lives.

Materials Needed

✳ copies of the reading assignment (pages 22–23)

✳ copies of the writing assignment (page 24)

✳ colorful picture of a parrot (*optional*)

Part I: The Reading Connection

A. Develop interest in the topic.

Ask the students to list animals that live in the jungle. Some common jungle animals are zebras, elephants, deer, birds, lions, and giraffes. Write these animals on the board so the students can see them and practice reading them.

B. Encourage students to make predictions about the reading.

1. Tell the students that they will be reading a story called "The Secret Teller." Explain that this story is an example of a fable. Tell students that fables are stories that teach a lesson. Explain that fables often use animals as the main characters.

2. Ask students to make predictions about the story. *Ask:* "Based on the title of the story and what you know about fables, what do you think this story might be about?" Allow students to give creative answers.

Part I: The Reading Connection *(cont.)*

C. Encourage good reading habits.

1. Remind students that as they read, they should picture what they are reading in their minds. In fact, they should be watching the story in their minds as if they were watching a television screen.

2. Have the students practice this skill. Have students shut their eyes as you read the following selection from the story to them:

> *Mr. Parrot heard the zebras tell their secrets as they ate the grass. He listened to the elephants as they played in the water. He could easily hear the lions talking. He would fly into the trees to hear the giraffes. He would sit on a branch and listen to the deer as they ate.*

3. Ask the students to describe the moving pictures in their minds. You might help them to develop their pictures by asking questions such as, "What does a jungle look like? What colors do you see? What is moving in your images? What sounds do you hear?"

4. Have the students shut their eyes again and have them repeat the exercise in order to practice this skill.

D. Establish a purpose for reading.

Pass out copies of "The Secret Teller" (pages 22–23) for the students to read. Read aloud the questions that the students should answer as they read the story:

1. What does Mr. Parrot tell the monkeys?

2. Why do the monkeys want to teach Mr. Parrot a lesson?

3. What lesson can you learn from the story?

4. Underline a sentence in the story that helps you to see the story in your mind.

E. Define and extend word meaning.

The word *parrot* is used in the story, and it might be a new word for some of the students. If possible, show the students a colorful picture of a parrot. You may choose to give your students the following description of parrots:

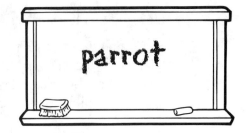

> *Parrots are birds with bright colors such as green, blue, orange, red, and yellow. Some parrots are able to say many words and phrases. Some people argue that parrots only say words and phrases without understanding what they are saying. Other people argue that a parrot can learn to understand words.*

Part I: The Reading Connection *(cont.)*

F. Allow ample time for students to read the story and complete the reading assignment.

G. Discuss the answers to the reading assignment together.

1. *What does Mr. Parrot tell the monkeys?* Mr. Parrot tells the monkeys the other animals' secrets.

2. *Why do the monkeys want to teach Mr. Parrot a lesson?* The monkeys do not think that Mr. Parrot should be telling the other animals' secrets to them.

3. *What lesson can you learn from the story?* From reading the story, you can learn to be careful with your secrets.

4. *Underline a sentence in the story that helps you to see the story in your mind.* Answers will vary. However, students should select sentences that offer some type of a description.

Part II: The Writing Connection

A. Develop interest in the topic.

Ask: "What are some important lessons that you have learned?" As students provide answers, list them on the board. (An example of a suitable answer might be, "keeping your neighborhood clean.")

B. Explain the writing assignment to the students.

Explain that the students are going to write a short fable. In their fables, they will teach a lesson that they have learned.

C. Assist students in organizing their mini-fables.

1. Provide students with the writing assignment handout on page 24.

2. Have students answer the "Get Some Idea" questions on their writing handout.

   ✱ What lesson have you learned?

   ✱ Where were you when you learned the lesson?

   ✱ Who taught you this lesson?

   ✱ How did you learn this lesson?

3. Then, remind the students that in fables, animals are often used as characters instead of people. Have the students select an animal to "be them," and another animal to be the person who helps them learn their lesson. Have them write those ideas on their handouts. (See the "Select Your Animal Characters" prompts.)

4. Finally, read aloud the sample mini-fable on the handout. Have the students use that as a model for their own mini-fables.

Part II: The Writing Connection *(cont.)*

D. Allow writing time.

Give students ample time to write their mini-fables. As they are working, walk around the room and offer guidance.

E. Give students a strategy to help them revise their writing.

Explain to the students that descriptive words are important. They allow someone else to see what they see in their minds. Descriptive words help writers to share their thoughts and ideas.

One way to add descriptive words in writing is to describe what something looks like. Read the following as an example and have the students listen for descriptive words:

Once there was a <u>shaggy, brown</u> dog that liked playing in a <u>large</u> neighborhood park. The <u>brown</u> dog learned to be friendly to new animals. The dog learned this lesson when she saw a <u>new, beautiful, yellow</u> and <u>blue</u> butterfly at the park. The <u>pretty</u> butterfly was sadly watching everyone play. But the butterfly was not playing. So the dog asked the butterfly to play. The butterfly was so happy. Today, the <u>shaggy, brown</u> dog and <u>beautiful, yellow</u> and <u>blue</u> butterfly are best friends.

Give students time to use this new skill to revise their work. Have the students reread their paragraphs and circle anything that could be described in more detail.

F. Give students a strategy to help them edit their writing.

Explain that when using words that describe, sometimes a comma is needed. One way to see if a comma is needed is to see if the word "and" sounds right in the description. If the word "and" sounds right, a comma is probably needed. For example, it should sound right to say, "a shaggy and brown dog." So it is correct to write, "a shaggy, brown dog." But it does not sound right to say, "a large and neighborhood park." So a comma would not be right there.

Have students give some examples from their work. Together as a class, decide if a comma is needed in the different examples.

Give students time to use this new skill to edit their work.

G. Publish students' ideas.

Have the students write a clean draft of their mini-fables. Have them draw a picture of an animal in the story to go along with their stories. Read a few of the stories aloud to the class. Display some of the stories in the school building.

The Reading Assignment

Directions: Read the fable "The Secret Teller" below and on page 23. After you are done, answer the questions on page 23.

The Secret Teller

Once upon a time, there was a bird that lived in a jungle. All the animals liked to talk to the bird. They thought he was so friendly. His name was Mr. Parrot. He liked to listen to everyone's secrets.

Mr. Parrot heard the zebras tell their secrets as they ate the grass. He listened to the elephants as they played in the water. He could easily hear the lions talking. He would fly into the trees to hear the giraffes. He would sit on a branch and listen to the deer as they ate. But he would tell everything he heard to the monkeys in the trees.

These monkeys were a bit tricky. They did not think that it was right for the bird to tell secrets. They wanted to teach the bird a lesson.

The monkeys asked all the animals for help. The next day, all the animals dressed up as monkeys.

Soon, Mr. Parrot flew near. He told the monkeys all the secrets he knew. He whispered the zebras' secrets. He hooted as he told the elephants' secrets. He roared the lions' secrets. He told the secrets of the giraffe and deer, too.

The Reading Assignment *(cont.)*

The Secret Teller *(cont.)*

As the animals heard their secrets, they took off their monkey masks. When Mr. Parrot was finished talking, he saw all of the animals of the forest. The next day, no one would talk to the bird.

Mr. Parrot apologized to all of the animals. He asked the animals not to tell him any secrets anymore. It was too hard for him to keep secrets, he explained.

"Yes," said the monkeys, "Be careful of your secrets." And this advice is still good today.

Answer the following questions:

1. What does Mr. Parrot tell the monkeys? _____

_____

_____

2. Why do the monkeys want to teach Mr. Parrot a lesson?_____

_____

_____

3. What lesson can you learn from the story? _____

_____

_____

_____

_____

4. Underline a sentence in the story that helps you to see the story in your mind.

The Writing Assignment

Write a mini-fable about a lesson that you learned. Here is an example of a mini-fable:

Once there was a dog that liked playing in a park. The dog learned to be friendly to new animals. The dog learned this lesson when she saw a new butterfly at the park. The butterfly was watching everyone play. But the butterfly was not playing. So the dog asked the butterfly to play. The butterfly was so happy. Today, the dog and butterfly are best friends.

Get Some Ideas

1. What lesson have you learned? _____

_____

2. Where were you when you learned the lesson? _____

3. Who helped you to learn this lesson? _____

4. How did you learn this lesson? _____

_____

Select Your Animal Characters

1. Instead of me, I will use _____.

2. Instead of the person teaching me the lesson, I will use _____

_____.

Your Mini-Fable

Once there was a _____ *that* _____

_____. *The* _____ *learned*

_____.

The _____ *learned this lesson when* _____

_____.

Today, _____

_____.

The Reading Connection

Teacher Directions: Evaluate the answers to the reading assignment

Objective	Possible Points	Earned Points
You understood the story.		
You understood the lesson that was taught in the fable.		
You underlined a sentence that could help you to picture the story in your mind.		
Total Earned Points:		

The Writing Connection

Teacher Direction: Evaluate the fables.

Objective	Possible Points	Earned Points
You clearly teach a lesson.		
You use animals as your characters.		
You tell where and how the lesson was learned.		
You put effort into using descriptive words, and using commas when needed.		
You put effort into the writing process.		
Total Earned Points:		

Additional Teacher Comments: _____

_____

_____

_____

Objectives

Reading

✔ To identify common ideas that are in myths around the world

✔ To sound out unknown words using letter sounds and letter combinations

Writing

✔ To write a myth

✔ To use dialogue

✔ To punctuate dialogue correctly

Lesson Summary

The students will read a myth called "The Sad Moon." Then, the students will write a myth of their own.

Materials Needed

✷ copies of the reading assignment (page 30)

✷ copies of the writing assignment (pages 31–32)

Part I: The Reading Connection

A. Develop interest in the topic.

Ask the following types of questions: "Why is the sky blue?" "Why do stars twinkle?" "Why do leaves turn colors in the autumn?" "Why does the wind blow?"

Ask: "What types of questions are these?" These are questions about the world around us. Encourage students to ask some of their own questions about the world.

B. Encourage students to make predictions about the reading.

1. Tell the students that they will be reading a story called "The Sad Moon." Explain that this story is an example of a myth. Teach students that myths are stories that try to answer questions about why things happen in the world the way they do. Often, gods and goddesses are the main characters in myths. Although some people may still believe in these gods and goddesses, these myths are most often referred to as "ancient beliefs" or old beliefs.

    Myths can be found in different cultures around the world. Many myths that are told today are very old. They were told even before stories were written down.

2. Ask students to make predictions about the story. *Ask:* "Based on the title of the story 'The Sad Moon' and what you know about myths, what do you think this story might be about?" Allow students to give creative answers.

Part I: The Reading Connection *(cont.)*

C. Encourage good reading habits.

Remind students that all good readers sometime see words that they have never seen before. One way good readers try to figure out how to say words is to sound out the words using what they know about sounds and different letter combinations.

Write the word "THOTH" on the board. Thoth is the Egyptian god of the moon. Use this word as an example. Students who have never seen this word can guess that the /th/ at the beginning and end of the word is blended together to make one sound.

D. Establish a purpose for reading.

Pass out copies of "The Sad Moon" (page 30) for the students to read. Read aloud the questions that the students should answer as they read the story.

1. What gods and goddesses are in this myth?

2. What question about the world is this myth trying to answer?

3. Circle a word that you needed to sound out in order to read it.

E. Define and extend word meaning.

The word *goddess* is used in the story, and it might be a new word for some of the students. Ask students to examine the word to look for a smaller word that they might know. Students should see the word *god*. "Goddess" refers to a female and "god" refers to a male.

F. Allow ample time for students to read the story and complete the reading assignment.

G. Discuss the answers to the reading assignment together.

1. *What gods and goddesses are in this myth?* The African goddess Arawa and the African god Adro are in this myth.

2. *What question about the world is this myth trying to answer?* The question that this myth is trying to answer is "Why are there stars in the sky?"

3. *Circle a word that you needed to sound out in order to read it.* Answers will vary, but students might choose to circle *Adro* or *Arawa*.

Part II: The Writing Connection

A. Develop interest in the topic.

Write the following questions on the board:

* ✱ "Why is the sky blue?"

* ✱ "Why do stars twinkle?"

* ✱ "Why do leaves turn colors in the autumn?"

* ✱ "Why does the wind blow?"

Remind students that myths are stories that try to give answers to questions like these—questions that ask about our world and the way things work in our world.

Have students ask more questions. List the students' questions on the board, as well.

B. Explain the writing assignment to the students.

Tell the students that they will be writing myths. They will write a short story that answers one of the questions that was just asked or a new question that they'd like to answer. Some of the characters in their stories should be gods and goddesses, just like in "ancient" or "olden day" myths. (On the student handout, there is a list of gods and goddesses from different ancient cultures.)

C. Assist students in organizing their descriptive paragraphs.

1. Distribute to students copies of the writing assignment on page 31.

2. Help the students gather their ideas. Lead them through the steps of identifying their myth's question and answer, selecting their gods and goddesses, and listing the main events in their stories. (Encourage students to be creative, but you might want to let them pick from the examples provided if they need some ideas.)

3. Remind students that they should tell where their gods and goddesses are from and what their gods and goddesses do.

D. Allow writing time.

Give students ample time to turn their ideas into myths. As they are working, walk around the room and offer guidance.

Part II: The Writing Connection *(cont.)*

E. Give students a strategy to help them revise their writing.

Explain that one way to make a character in a story interesting is to make the character talk. When characters in a play or story speak, it is called dialogue.

Read "The Sad Moon" aloud to the students. Have the students raise their hands when they hear the dialogue.

Give students time to add dialogue into their own stories.

F. Give students a strategy to help them edit their writing.

Remind students that there is certain punctuation that is used to let readers know when a character is talking.

✷ Quotation marks are put before the first word being said and after the last word.

✷ Ending punctuation is put inside the quotation marks.

Example: "Why are you sad?" Adro, the sky god, asked.

Note to the Classroom Teacher: Punctuating dialogue can get complicated for students. Depending on the ability of the students and their experience using dialogue, you might want to discuss the punctuation inside the quotes, as well as the punctuation that follows. (There is a period at the end of the sentence, even if a question is being asked.) Or, you might just want to focus on the punctuation within the quotes for this exercise.

To extend their knowledge, if you think your students are ready, you might want to show them what dialogue looks like if the speaker is identified at the end of the quote (like in the above example), plus what dialogue looks like if the speaker is identified before the quote.

Example: Arawa answered, "I am sad because I am lonely."

G. Publish students' ideas.

Make a book with all the students' myths. Give the book to the media center to display for a period of time.

The Reading Assignment

Directions: Read "The Sad Moon" and answer the questions below.

The Sad Moon

Arawa, the African goddess of the moon, was very happy. Each night, she lit up the sky. People on Earth would look up to her and say, "Ah, there is the moon. Isn't she beautiful?"

One night, Arawa grew sad. That was a very dark night for Earth, for no moon lit up the sky that night. Adro, the African god of the sky, went to visit Arawa.

"Why are you sad?" Adro asked.

Arawa answered, "I am sad because I am lonely. I am the only light in the night sky."

"I can help you, Arawa. I will give you friends that will shine with you during the night. They will not be as bright as you, but they will keep you company." So, Adro added stars to the sky. Arawa was happy. The moon lit up the sky once more.

Answer the following questions:

1. What gods and goddesses are in this myth? _____

   _____

   _____

2. What question about the world is this myth trying to answer? _____

   _____

   _____

   _____

3. Circle a word that you needed to sound out in order to read it.

Lesson Four

The Writing Assignment

Directions: Write a myth. Your myth should answer a question about the world around us. Your myth should have gods and goddesses as some of the characters, just like "ancient" or old myths.

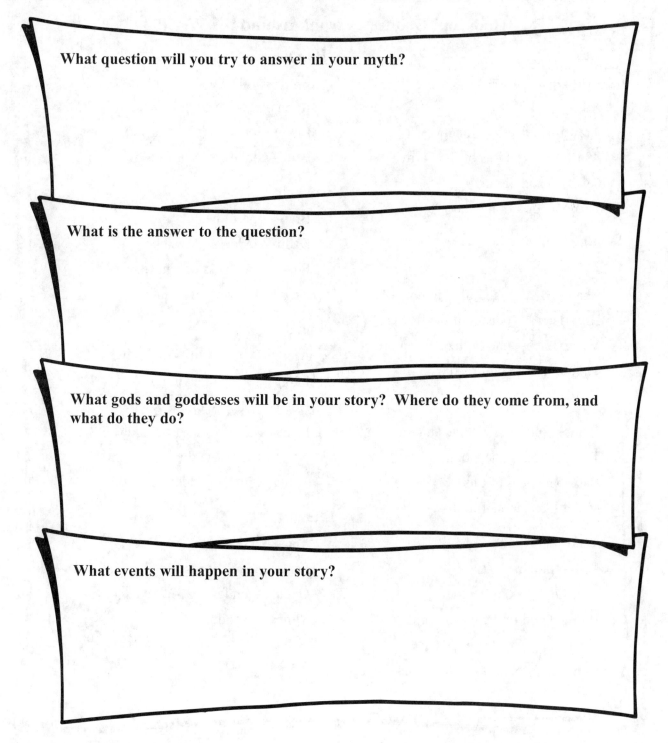

What question will you try to answer in your myth?

What is the answer to the question?

What gods and goddesses will be in your story? Where do they come from, and what do they do?

What events will happen in your story?

Directions: Use the list below to help you create your myth.

Gods and Goddesses from Around the World

Africa

Abzu—god of water

Adro—god of sky

Arawa—goddess of the moon

Asase Ya—goddess of the Earth

Gwalu—god of rain

Shango—god of thunder

China

Ao—god of the sea

Chang Hs'ien—god of children

Hua-Hsien—goddess of the flower

Meng-T'ien—god of the writing brush

Yao-Wang—god of medicine

Egypt

Hathor—goddess of love and music

Thoth—god of the moon

Bast—goddess of cats

Ma'at—goddess of truth

Greece

Zeus—king of gods

Poseiden—god of the sea

Hades—god of the underworld

Hera—queen of the gods

Demeter—goddess of grains and crops

Hawaii

Kane—god of forest and trees

Kapua—god of troublemakers

Laka—goddess of clouds and storms

Pele—goddess of volcano fires

Ireland

Bran—god of health

Danu—goddess of water

Flidais—goddess of nature

Angus Og—god of beauty

Japan

Amatsu-Mikaboshi—god of evil

Fujin—god of the wind

Hotei—god of happiness

Kura-Okami—god of rain and snow

Nai-no-Kami—god of earthquakes

Tatsuta-hime—goddess of autumn

Rome

Mars—god of war

Pan—god of the woods

Cupid—goddess of love

Minerva—goddess of wisdom

Vulcan — god of fire

The Reading Connection

Teacher Directions: Evaluate the answers to the reading questions.

Objective	Possible Points	Earned Points
You identified the gods and goddesses in the myth.		
You identified the question that the myth was trying to answer.		
You circled a word that you had to sound out during your reading.		
Total Earned Points:		

The Writing Connection

Teacher Direction: Evaluate the myths.

Objective	Possible Points	Earned Points
Your myth answered a question about the world around you.		
You picked gods and goddesses for your characters. You told who they were.		
You made characters speak (dialogue).		
You punctuated the dialogue correctly.		
You put effort into the writing process.		
Total Earned Points:		

Additional Teacher Comments: _____

_____

_____

_____

Lesson Five

Objectives

Reading

✔ To use researching skills to learn about folktales

✔ To use more than one text when researching information

✔ To pick important facts to record while researching

✔ To use titles to make guesses about books

Writing

✔ To write a paragraph about folktales

✔ To paraphrase facts

✔ To select a direct quote

✔ To use an introductory sentence

✔ To cite sources

Lesson Summary

The students will use sample texts to research and learn about folktales. Then, the students will write a paragraph informing others what they learned through research about folktales.

Materials Needed

✱ copies of the reading assignment (pages 39–40)

✱ copies of the writing assignment (pages 41–42)

Part I: The Reading Connection

A. Develop interest in the topic.

Ask: "What do the following have in common: fables, fairy tales, legends, myths, and tall tales?" Accept reasonable answers, but point out that all these different types of stories are folktales. Teach students that *folktale* is a general term to describe stories told by people. Folktales were told before people even wrote stories down. They were passed down through the generations by people telling them from memory. They are a very old form of entertainment and education.

Explain that the students are going to do some research to learn about folktales. Ask students what they already know about the research process. Teach students that the reason people do research is to learn information about something.

Part I: The Reading Connection *(cont.)*

B. Encourage students to make predictions about the reading.

Ask students to make predictions about their research task. *Ask:* "What might you learn from your research about folktales today?" Answers will vary. For example, students might predict that they will learn the definition of a folktale, what some examples of folktales are, who wrote folktales, or how to write a folktale.

C. Encourage good reading habits.

Remind students that readers make guesses about what they are going to read. One way that readers can make guesses about what they are going to read is to look at the title of the material. Titles can give many different clues.

Ask: "If you were reading a book called *The Dark and Stormy Night*, what guesses could you make?" Answers will vary. Students might guess that the story will take place on a dark and stormy night, that it is a mystery or a scary story, or that it is a story about nature.

D. Establish a purpose for reading.

Distribute pages 39–40 to students. Ask students to look at the titles of the three books they are going to use for their research.

Then ask the following questions:

✳ "What questions might I ask you to answer while you are researching folktales?"

✳ "What is a folktale?"

✳ "What are different kinds of folktales?"

✳ "Who wrote folktales?"

E. Define and extend word meaning.

The word *exaggerated* is used in the reading, and it might be a new word for some of the students. As an example, exaggerate for the students. Say something like, "I was so tired yesterday that I fell asleep right in the middle of the grocery store." *Exaggerated* means "made to seem much greater or more than it really is."

Part I: The Reading Connection *(cont.)*

F. Allow ample time for students to research information and take notes on what they learn by answering the questions.

Remind students that when they research, they will learn a lot of information. They will need to decide how much information they really need. They don't need to record every fact that they find.

G. Discuss the answers to the reading assignment together.

Answers will vary because a lot of information was provided. Sample answers are included here.

1. *What is a folktale?* A folktale is a story about a person's beliefs or worries, or a story about the world.

2. *What are different kinds of folktales?* Different kinds of folktales are fables, fairy tales, legends, and tall tales.

3. *Who wrote folktales?* We do not know the original authors of most folktales, but some famous authors who wrote folktales were the Brothers Grimm and Joel Chandler Harris.

Part II: The Writing Connection

A. Develop interest in the topic.

1. *Ask:* "Who says, 'I'll huff and I'll puff and I'll blow your house down'?" The big bad wolf says this.

Explain that this is an example of a direct quote. These are the exact words that the big bad wolf says. *Ask:* "What other direct quotes do you know?" Have students share with you other famous direct quotes that they know or direct quotes that their friends or family members have said.

Explain that people do research to learn new information. Then, people write down their research to tell others what they have learned. When writing about research, sometimes people use the exact words that they read during their research. They use direct quotes.

When using a direct quote, you must put quotation marks around the words to show that they are not your own words. (Point out that writers can't use too many direct quotes in their writing. If they use too many direct quotes, someone else has done the writing, not them.)

Lesson
Five

Part II: The Writing Connection *(cont.)*

A. Develop interest in the topic. *(cont.)*

2. Then, explain that Cinderella says something about dreams coming true. Explain that these were not Cinderella's exact words. When you put someone else's words into your own words, it is called paraphrasing. Ask student to paraphrase things that famous people have said or that their friends or family members have said.

Explain that when writing about research, most of what they will need to do is to paraphrase. They will need to take the ideas from their research and put them into their own words.

B. Explain the writing assignment to the students.

Each student will need a copy of "The Reading Assignment" on pages 39–40 and "The Writing Assignment" on pages 41–42. Explain to the students that they will use information from three different books to write a paragraph about folktales. (The sources that the students will use are provided on the handouts.)

Direct the students to the requirements of the writing assignment. Each student should do the following:

✳ Answer the question, "What is a folktale?"

✳ Use at least six facts.

✳ Use at least one fact from each of the three books.

✳ Paraphrase five pieces of information.

✳ Use one direct quote.

C. Assist students in organizing their descriptive paragraphs.

Lead the students through the directions on the writing assignment handout (pages 41–42) to help them gather their facts for their paragraphs. Have the students:

✳ Underline six facts within the reading material.

✳ Paraphrase five facts.

✳ Use one direct quote.

D. Allow writing time.

Give students ample time to write their paragraphs. As they are working, walk around the room and offer guidance.

Part II: The Writing Connection *(cont.)*

E. Give students a strategy to help them revise their writing.

Explain to the students that there are different reasons to write. One reason to write is to share information. That is what they are doing with their paragraphs about folktales.

A good way to start a paragraph that gives information is to tell the reader what information you are about to give. (This is called an introductory sentence or topic sentence.)

Write the following examples on the board:

✳ There is a lot to know about folktales.

✳ Folktales are important.

✳ By studying folktales, we can learn about people.

✳ Folktales are very interesting.

Have students select one of these or write their own topic sentences.

F. Give students a strategy to help them edit their writing.

Remind students that when they take information from somewhere, they must "thank" the person who gave them the information. In this case, students must say "thank you" to the people who wrote and published the books that they used. This is called *citing a source*. Teach students that it is important to cite sources. When sources are not cited, it is called *plagiarism*. *Plagiarism* is taking other people's words or ideas.

Teach students how to cite a source using the information provided on their handouts (pages 39–40). Completed sources should look like this:

Tories, S. *What Is a Folktale?* Peoria: Long Ago Publishing Company, 1905.

Tales, Fare E. *Different Kinds of Folktales.* Baltimore: Folklore Publishers, 1881.

Nose, Hew. *Who Wrote Fairytales?* Wichita: Ye Old Press, 1925.

(**Note:** The method presented here is from the *MLA Handbook for Writers of Research Papers.* You may wish to teach a different method to your students.)

Have students either recopy this information under their paragraphs or attach the handout to their paragraphs.

G. Publish students' papers.

Display the students' papers in the library in the sections with folktales.

Lesson Five

The Reading Assignment

Directions: Read the following information about folktales.

The following passage is from page 5 of *What Is a Folktale?*, which was written by S. Tories in 1905. This book was published in Peoria, IL, by Long Ago Publishing Company.

The word *folk* means "people." The word *tale* means "story." Folktales are stories told by people. Folktales are told all over the world. They were told a long time ago. They were told before people could even write.

Folktales tell stories about beliefs that people had. They tell stories about things that *worry* people. Folktales also try to tell why the world is the way that it is.

This passage is from page 956 of *Who Wrote Folktales*? This book was written by Hew Nose and published in 1925 by Ye Old Press of Wichita, KS.

People began telling folktales a long time ago. People told folktales before the time of books. They were told to children, and friends. Then they were told to other children, friends, families, and travelers. That is how the stories spread. They were fun to tell and fun to hear. We do not know who told the very old folktales.

When books were invented, people began to write down folktales. Some of the folktales that people wrote down were very old stories. People also wrote new stories.

There are some famous people who are known for writing down folktales. Aesop is known for his fables. Joel Chandler Harris is known for his animal stories. The Grimm Brothers are known for their fairy tales. Washington Irving is known for his legends. Mark Twain wrote tall tales. Homer wrote some very long myths.

The Reading Assignment *(cont.)*

Directions: Read the following information about folktales.

The following description is from page 23 of Fare E. Tales's 1881 book entitled *Different Kinds of Folktales*. This book was published in Baltimore, MD, by Folklore Publishers.

Have you ever read a fable? Have you ever heard a fairy tale? Do you know what a legend is? Have you ever told a tall tale? Have you ever studied myths? Well, these are all folktales. Folktales describe many kinds of stories.

Fables are stories that teach lessons. The characters in fables are animals. One fable is "The Tortoise and the Hare."

Fairy tales are stories that have magic, royalty, castles, and pretend animals. One fairy tale is "Sleeping Beauty."

Legends are stories about heroes. "The Legend of Sleepy Hollow" is a legend.

Tall tales are stores with heroes, too. Tall tales usually have funny parts in them. Often, something is exaggerated in a tall tale. "Davy Crockett" is a tall tale.

Myths are stories that try to explain the world around us. Myths have gods and goddesses in the stories. "Jason and the Golden Fleece" is a myth.

Lesson Five

The Writing Assignment

Directions: Write a paragraph about folktales.

* Use at least *six* facts.

* Use *three* books.

* Paraphrase *five* pieces of information. (*Paraphrase* means "to put someone else's words into your own words.")

* Use *one* direct quote. (A *direct quote* is the exact words that someone else said or wrote.)

A. Underline *six* facts that you would like to use in your paragraph. Use information from each book.

B. Paraphrase *five* of the facts that you have underlined.

1. _____

   _____

2. _____

   _____

3. _____

   _____

4. _____

   _____

5. _____

   _____

C. Pick one direct quote.

   _____

   _____

The Writing Assignment *(cont.)*

D. Write your paragraph.

_____

_____

_____

_____

_____

_____

_____

E. Cite the sources you used while researching. Follow this format:

Author's Last Name, Author's First Name. <u>Title of Book.</u> City of Publication: Publisher, Date of Publication.

1. _____

_____

2. _____

_____

3. _____

_____

Lesson Five

The Reading Connection

Teacher Directions: Evaluate the "Question and Answer" section of the reading handout.

Objective	Possible Points	Earned Points
You used titles to make guesses about what three books were about.		
You picked facts that were needed for your research.		
Total Earned Points:		

The Writing Connection

Teacher Direction: Evaluate the paragraphs, and the cited sources.

Objective	Possible Points	Earned Points
You started your paragraph with a strong sentence.		
You paraphrased five facts.		
You used one direct quote.		
You used facts from three books, and you cited them.		
You put effort into the writing process.		
Total Earned Points:		

Additional Teacher Comments: _____

_____

_____

_____

Objectives

Reading

✔ To define the word *persuade*

✔ To understand why readers should know when they are reading something persuasive

✔ To understand ways of finding persuasive writing

Writing

✔ To identify ways to persuade others

✔ To write a friendly letter using a correct format

Lesson Summary

The students will read a persuasive friendly letter. This letter tries to convince students that having an ice cream party is not a good idea. Then, the students will write a persuasive friendly letter trying to convince the teacher that having an ice cream party is a good idea.

Materials Needed

✶ copies of the reading assignment (page 48)

✶ copies of the writing assignment (pages 49–50)

✶ ice cream (*optional—but a fun option to culminate the lesson*)

Part I: The Reading Connection

A. **Develop interest in the topic.**

Say: "Pretend that you were trying to persuade me to have an ice cream party. What would you say to try to persuade me to organize it?" Answers will vary. Lead students away from begging (e.g., "Please!") and encourage them to come up with reasons why they deserve an ice cream party. Ask questions such as the following: "Do you study hard? Do you put effort into my class? Do you treat me politely? Do you treat others in the class politely?"

(**Note:** If you are not going to give students ice cream, make it clear to them that this is a pretend topic. Explain that you are just using this topic to teach them about persuasion.)

Lesson Six

Part I: The Reading Connection *(cont.)*

B. Encourage students to make predictions about the reading.

Tell students that they will be reading a letter that will try to persuade them to understand why having an ice cream party is not a good idea. *Ask:* "What reasons might I use to try to persuade you that having an ice cream party is not a good idea?" Answers will vary. Students might guess that the letter will say that ice cream is messy, will melt easily, or has too much sugar.

C. Encourage good reading habits; define and extend word meaning.

Remind students that one reason that people write is to try to persuade other people to agree with them. Ask the following questions:

✳ **What does *persuade* mean?** *Persuade* means "to try to get others to agree with an idea."

✳ **Who writes things down to try to persuade you to do things?** Answers might include advertisers on television, magazine advertisements, or one's parents (e.g., notes left on the counter listing reasons why you should clean your room).

✳ **Why is it important for you to understand when you are reading something persuasive?** Persuasive writing might be wrong, it might be an opinion (not fact), or it might show only facts that will help make one side of the argument stronger.

✳ **What could the problem be if someone reads something persuasive and does not realize it is persuasive?** The problem with reading something persuasive and not knowing it is persuasive is that the reader could think that the information is correct and/or that it is the only way to look at something.

✳ **How can you tell when you are reading something persuasive?** Persuasive writers will try to get you to agree by giving you reasons why his or her argument is right.

The word *persuaded* appears in the reading. Students may never have seen this word. Write the word on the board and help the students learn to decode the word.

D. Establish a purpose for reading.

Pass out copies of page 48 for the students to read. Read aloud the question that the students should answer as they read the story.

Question: What reasons does the letter give for not having an ice cream party?

Part I: The Reading Connection *(cont.)*

E. Allow ample time for students to read the story and complete the reading assignment.

F. Discuss the answers to the reading assignment together.

Question: What reasons does the letter give for not having an ice cream party?

✴ Ice cream has sugar. Sugar is not good for teeth.

✴ Ice cream is messy and could make the classroom sticky.

✴ There are many different kinds of ice cream. The teacher would not know what kind to get.

Part II: The Writing Connection

A. Develop interest in the topic.

Read the letter on page 48 aloud to the students. Review with your students the following questions from page 45:

✴ What does *persuade* mean?

✴ Who writes things down to try to persuade you to do things?

✴ Why is it important for you to understand when you are reading something persuasive?

✴ What could the problem be if someone reads something persuasive and does not realize it is persuasive?

✴ How can you tell when you are reading something persuasive?

B. Explain the writing assignment to the students.

Tell students that they are going to be writing a friendly letter to their teacher, trying to persuade him or her to allow an ice cream party.

C. Assist students in organizing their persuasive letters.

Distribute copies of the writing assignment on pages 49–50 to students. Help the students gather their ideas. *Ask:* "What are some reasons that you think you should have an ice cream party?" Write student responses on board. Students can select from this list, or they can create their own reasons. Have them write their selected reasons on their handout. (There is a chart on the student handout. The chart will be addressed during the revision process.)

D. Allow writing time.

Give students ample time to begin writing their letters. As they are working, walk around the room offering guidance.

Part II: The Writing Connection *(cont.)*

E. Give students a strategy to help them revise their writing.

Explain to the students that sometimes when writers revise they look for places to add information. When doing persuasive writing, writers should look to see where they can make their argument stronger. One way to make a persuasive argument stronger is to figure out what people would say in an argument against your point. For example, what reasons did the letter already give for not wanting a party? Write those reasons on the chart (page 49).

Next, discuss each point so that it does not hurt your argument. For example, ice cream has some sugar, but a little bit of sugar is not unhealthy. Plus, there is sugarless ice cream that the teacher could pick.

Have students complete their charts. Then, allow students time to revise their letters, using this new persuasive skill. Give students time to address at least one of the teacher's concerns in their letters.

F. Give students a strategy to help them edit their writing.

Place page 48 on the overhead. Identify the different parts of the friendly letter. Have students format their letters to look the same as this one. Point out the following:

* Indent the sender's return address.

* Skip a line after the return address and indent the date.

* Add the greeting, and follow it with a comma. (Dear _____ ,)

* Skip a line, indent, and begin each paragraph.

* Indent the closing (e.g., Sincerely, Yours truly, Thank you, etc.) and follow it with a comma.

* Handwrite a signature.

* Print the name of the sender.

Give students time to edit, using the new skill.

G. Publish students' ideas.

Have students select their strongest persuasive paragraph from their letters. Have students read that paragraph aloud to the class.

The Reading Assignment

Directions: Read the friendly letter below. Then answer the question that follows.

32 Iceberg Way

Cold Spring, New York 10516

December 23, This Year

Dear Class,

We have had a very good year. We have worked well together. We have gotten to know one another. We all have learned many new things. Hard work and learning are both reasons to celebrate.

I heard that you wanted to celebrate by having an ice cream party. But I do not think that having an ice cream party is a good idea at all.

I have a few reasons why I do not think we should have an ice cream party. First, ice cream has a lot of sugar. Sugar is not good for your teeth. Also, ice cream is very messy when it melts. I don't want my classroom to be sticky. Third, there are many different kinds of ice cream. I wouldn't know what kind of ice cream to buy.

In closing, I don't think that we should have an ice cream party. I hope I have persuaded you to give up the idea.

Sincerely,

Your Teacher

Your Teacher

P.S. Please write back.

Answer the following question:

What reasons does the letter give for *not* having an ice cream party? _____

_____

_____

The Writing Assignment

Directions: Complete the "Think and Write" section below. Then complete the chart that follows.

Think and Write

Why is having an ice cream party in class a good idea? _____

_____

_____

_____

What problems did your teacher list with having an ice cream party?	What can you say about the problems that your teacher listed?

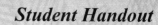 
The Writing Assignment *(cont.)*

Directions: Write a persuasive letter to your teacher about having an ice cream party in class.

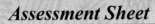 
Lesson Six

The Reading Connection

Teacher Directions: Evaluate the answers to the reading question.

Objective	Possible Points	Earned Points
You found the persuasive reasons listed in the letter.		
Total Earned Points:		

The Writing Connection

Teacher Direction: Evaluate the letter.

Objective	Possible Points	Earned Points
You gave reasons to make your argument strong.		
You solved at least one problem that your teacher presented.		
Format: You put effort into writing a friendly letter.		
You put effort into the writing process.		
Total Earned Points:		

Additional Teacher Comments: _____

_____

_____

_____

_____

_____

Making Personal Connections　　Lesson Seven　　**Teacher Instructions**

Objectives

Reading

✔ To personally connect with characters, events, feelings, and places while reading a story

Writing

✔ To connect personal experiences, events, and feelings to those in a story
✔ To tell a story with a beginning, middle, and end
✔ To use paragraphs purposefully and correctly

Lesson Summary

The students will read a story called "The Buttons." Then, students will learn to make personal connections to the story. Finally, students will write a true story that reminds them of a character, event, place, or feeling in "The Buttons."

Materials Needed

✳ copies of the reading assignment (pages 57–58)
✳ copies of the writing assignment (pages 59–60)
✳ copies of the "Common Storytelling Words" half-sheet (page 56)
✳ crayons or colored pencils (*optional*)

Part I: The Reading Connection

A. Develop interest in the topic.

Ask every student to sketch a picture of a button. Encourage students to be creative. Ask the following questions:

✳ What size is your button?
✳ What shape is your button?
✳ How many holes does your button have?
✳ Is this a button for a dress?

✳ Is it a button for a pillow?
✳ Is your button fancy or simple?
✳ Is it thick or thin?
✳ Is it stripped, solid, or polka-dotted?

It would be fun to give the students colored pencils or crayons to use when creating their buttons, but it is not necessary. If you don't want students to actually draw the buttons, you could ask students to imagine and describe their buttons to the class.

B. Encourage students to make predictions about the reading.

1. Tell the students that they will be reading a story called "The Buttons."

2. Ask students to make predictions about the story. *Ask:* "Based on the title of the story, what do you think this story could be about?" Allow students to give creative answers. Students might guess that the story is about something being sewn or about a family with the last name of Buttons.

#8032 Ready to Go Lessons: Grade 3　　52　　*©Teacher Created Resources, Inc.*

Part I: The Reading Connection *(cont.)*

C. Encourage good reading habits.

Tell students that when reading a story, readers can try to connect their own lives and experiences to those in the story. They can try to connect to . . .

✴ a *character* by thinking of similar people they know

✴ an *event* by thinking of similar things they have experienced

✴ a *place* by thinking of similar places they have been to or seen pictures of

✴ a *feeling* by thinking of similar feelings that they have had

For example, if they are reading a story that takes place in a classroom, they could picture a classroom that they have seen. If they are reading about a character who is excited, they can remember a time when they were excited. By connecting their own lives to a story they are reading, they can do the following:

✴ better picture the story in their minds.

✴ begin to understand why the characters do what they do, feel the way they feel, or act the way they act.

For example, you might be able to understand why a sad character started to cry in a story if you remember a time when you were sad and started to cry.

D. Establish a purpose for reading.

Pass out copies of "The Buttons" (pages 57–58) for the students to read. Read aloud the questions that the students should answer as they read the story.

E. Define and extend word meaning.

The word *project* is used in the story, and it might be a new word for some of the students to read. Before asking student to complete the reading assignment, write the word on the board. Help the students read the word. Then, use the following description to help the students understand the meaning of the word:

A project is something that takes more than one step to complete or is not simple to complete. For example, cleaning out your closet might be a project because you might have to figure out which clothes fit, which clothes you want to keep, which clothes are clean enough to leave in the closet, where all the toys are going to go, and where to place all of your shoes.

F. Allow ample time for students to read the story and complete the reading assignment.

Part I: The Reading Connection *(cont.)*

G. Discuss the answers to the reading assignment together.

1. *Why does Grant feel excited in the story?* Grant feels excited because he is going to do a special project in school. He is going to use buttons from home which he carefully picked out himself.

2. *Why does Grant feel enjoyment in the story?* Grant feels enjoyment picking out the buttons from his mother's button basket. He also enjoys the sounds the buttons make as he dumps them onto the floor.

3. *Why does Grant feel proud in the story?* Grant feels proud because he took time to pick out the perfect buttons for his special project.

4. *Why does Grant feel disappointment in the story?* Grant feels disappointment in the story because his special buttons were taken away and he does not like the new buttons that he was given.

5. *What other feeling could Grant have in the story? Why do you think he could feel that way?* Answers will vary. Grant might have felt anger at the teacher for taking his buttons, sadness for having lost his buttons, or hurt because the teacher did not understand that the buttons were important to him.

6. *When have you felt an emotion that Grant felt in the story?* Answers will vary.

7. *How can you personally connect to a place in the story?* The students have probably been in a classroom or on the floor of a home.

8. *How can you personally connect to an event in the story?* Answers will vary. Students might have looked forward to a special project in school, or they might have had someone do something that disappointed them.

9. *How can you personally connect to a character in a story?* Answers will vary, but students might either know someone younger who reminds them of Grant in the story or they might know someone who reminds them of the teacher in the story.

H. Practice the skill.

After answering these questions, you might want to reread the story aloud to the students and have them practice making connections to the story as you read to them. Then, you might want to continue the discussion. Answers will vary.

10. *When has someone hurt your feelings without meaning to do so? When did this happen in the story?*

11. *What reason might the teacher have had for collecting the buttons?*

12. *We do not know if Grant ever told the teacher how he felt. Have you ever hid your feelings? If so, why?*

Part II: The Writing Connection

A. Develop interest in the topic.

Have the students think about a movie or TV show that they have recently seen or a story that they recently read. Have them think about and discuss how it started, what happened in the middle, and how it ended.

Read "The Buttons" aloud to the students if you have not done so already. As the students listen, have them think about how it starts, what happens as it continues, and how it ends.

After reading the story, discuss with the students that "The Buttons" begins with a little boy excitedly coming to class with buttons for a project. In the story, the teacher then mixes up the buttons and returns different buttons to the boy, which he does not like. The story ends with a disappointed little boy who is no longer excited about the class project.

Teach students that when telling a story, there is usually a beginning, a middle, and an end.

B. Explain the writing assignment to the students.

Explain to the students that they will be writing a true story that reminds them of a character, event, place, or feeling in "The Buttons." For example, the little boy in the story felt disappointed when the teacher took his buttons, and so a student might choose to write about a time that he/she felt disappointed.

C. Assist students in organizing their descriptive paragraphs.

Distribute copies of pages 59–60 to students. Help the students gather their ideas. Read aloud the questions on their writing assignment handout and allow students time to answer each question. As students begin to gather their ideas, have them share them with the class. This might help struggling students come up with a connection for their stories.

The questions and answers on the reading handout (page 58) can be used to help students identify a topic for their stories as well.

D. Allow writing time.

Give students ample time to write their paragraphs. As they are working, walk around the room and offer guidance.

E. Give students a strategy to help them revise their writing.

Remind students that their stories should have a beginning, middle, and end. Explain that there are some words that can help the story flow from the beginning to the middle to the end.

Hand out the "Common Storytelling Words" half-sheet (on page 56). Have students use at least three of these words (or similar words) in their stories.

Part II: The Writing Connection *(cont.)*

F. Give students a strategy to help them edit their writing.

Show students the story "The Buttons." Have them count the different paragraphs that were written. ("The Buttons" has five paragraphs.) Explain that writers use different paragraphs to help a reader understand the story. Sometimes, a new paragraphs tells the reader that something new is happening in the story.

You can start a new paragraph to show a change in the following areas:

* action/event
* character
* time

* place
* mood
* description

Show students how to indent a paragraph. Give students time to edit their papers using this skill.

G. Publish students' ideas.

Read some of the students papers aloud. (You might want to change names of characters since students are writing about themselves.) Have students identify how the different stories relate to the story "The Buttons."

Common Storytelling Words

Beginning Story Words and Phrases

* Once there was . . .
* It all began when . . .

* One day . . .
* There was a time when . . .

Middle-of-the-Story Words and Phrases

* Then . . .
* After that . . .
* Soon . . .
* Next . . .

* There was also . . .
* Also . . .
* The next day . . .
* Several days later . . .

Ending Story Words and Phrases

* In the end, . . .
* So, . . .
* At the end of the day, . . .
* When it was all over . . .
* When it was time to leave . . .

* Finally . .
* Later . . .
* Since . . .
* After that . . .
* Afterward . . .

The Reading Assignment

Directions: Read the story "The Buttons" below. Answer the questions on page 58.

The Buttons

A small boy named Grant ran into the classroom with ten buttons in his hand. He was so excited. His teacher had asked everyone to bring in ten buttons from home. They needed the buttons for a special project.

Grant spent a long time picking his buttons. His mother had a special button basket. In the basket were many different buttons. There were small buttons and big buttons. There were simple buttons and fancy buttons. There were even smooth buttons and bumpy buttons.

Grant dumped all the buttons onto the floor. He liked the sound they made as they fell out of the basket. He wanted to see each button. The little buttons that came off his Dad's shirts he did not like. He liked the colorful buttons from his mother's sweaters. He took his time picking just the right ones for school.

Soon it was time for the special project. The teacher told everyone to take out his or her buttons. Grant proudly placed each of his buttons on his desk. The teacher came around the room and took the buttons. She placed them in a bag and shook them up. Then she gave every child ten different buttons. Grant ended up with all little buttons, just like the little buttons that came off of his Dad's shirts.

In the end, Grant did not think that the project was so special. In fact, Grant did not like the project at all. He just wanted his buttons back.

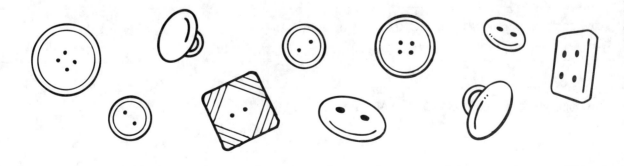

Lesson Seven

The Reading Assignment *(cont.)*

Directions: After reading "The Buttons," answer the questions below.

1. Why does Grant feel excited in the story? _____

_____

_____

2. Why does Grant feel enjoyment in the story? _____

_____

_____

3. Why does Grant feel proud in the story? _____

_____

_____

4. Why does Grant feel disappointment in the story? _____

_____

_____

5. What other feeling could Grant have in the story? Why do you think he could feel that way?

_____

_____

6. When have you felt an emotion that Grant felt in the story? _____

_____

_____

7. How can you personally connect to a place in the story? _____

_____

_____

8. How can you personally connect to an event in the story? _____

_____

_____

9. How can you personally connect to a character in a story? _____

_____

_____

The Writing Assignment

Directions: Choose a character, event, place, or feeling in "The Buttons" that reminds you of . . .

* someone you know
* something that happened to you

* somewhere that you have been
* a feeling that you've had

1. **What person, event, place, or feeling did you choose?**

2. **How does your story start?**

3. **What happens in the middle of your story?**

4. **How does your story end?**

The Writing Assignment *(cont.)*

Directions: In the frame below, write a true story about a person, event, place, or feeling. Use the common storytelling words and your answers to the questions on page 59 to help you.

Lesson
Seven

The Reading Connection

Teacher Directions: Evaluate the answers to the reading questions.

Objective	Possible Points	Earned Points
You thought about your own life to help you understand a story.		
Total Earned Points:		

The Writing Connection

Teacher Directions: Evaluate the narrative story.

Objective	Possible Points	Earned Points
You wrote a story that reminds you of a story we read in class. The stories have a similar character, feeling, place, or event.		
You used special storytelling words to help tell your story.		
Your indented new paragraphs.		
Your story had a beginning, middle, and ending.		
You put effort into the writing process.		
Total Earned Points:		

Additional Teacher Comments: _____

_____

_____

_____

_____

Objectives

Reading

✔ To identify common patterns authors use to tell information (compare/contrast, cause/effect, time order, idea/support, problem/solution)

Writing

✔ To write a persuasive, friendly letter using common patterns of telling information (compare/contrast, cause/effect, time order, idea/support, problem/solution)

✔ To write a friendly letter in the correct format

✔ To choose words to write for a specific person (audience)

Lesson Summary

The students will read a story called "Maxwell's Plan." Then, students will identify common organizational patterns that the author uses to tell information. Students will write a persuasive letter telling their ideas for a relaxing time, using the common organizational patterns of telling information.

Materials Needed

✳ copies of the reading assignment (pages 67–68)

✳ copies of the writing assignment (pages 69–70)

✳ handout or overhead of "Friendly Letter" (page 71)

Part I: The Reading Connection

A. Develop interest in the topic.

Ask students if they ever helped plan something. For example, did they ever help plan a party, trip, menu, shopping list, or a day? Let students share their experiences.

B. Encourage students to make predictions about the reading.

1. Tell the students that they will be reading a story called "Maxwell's Plan."

2. Ask students to make predictions about the story. *Ask:* "Based on the title of the story, what do you think this story might be about?" Allow students to give creative answers.

Part I: The Reading Connection *(cont.)*

C. Encourage good reading habits.

Explain that many times, authors give information in patterns. Some common patterns are as follows:

✳ **Compare and Contrast**—Writers tell how things are the same and how they are different.
Example: Chris has blond hair. Dan has brown hair. Both boys are the same age.

✳ **Time Order**—Writers tell things in the order that they happened or will happen.
Example: First, I ate a lollipop, and then I drank a soda.

✳ **Cause and Effect**—Writers tell how or why something happened or will happen.
Example: If you go to school, you will learn new things.

✳ **Idea and Support**—Writers tell an idea, and then explain the idea.
Example: I need to go to the store because I am out of milk.

✳ **Problem and Solution**—Writers tell a problem and then tell how to solve the problem.
Example: I am hungry, so I should eat a snack.

Explain that these patterns can be found in all sorts of writing. They can be found in stories, textbooks, newspapers, etc. Encourage students to try to find these different patterns in "Maxwell's Plan."

D. Establish a purpose for reading.

Pass out copies of "Maxwell's Plan" (pages 67–68) for the students to read. Read aloud the questions that the students should answer as they read the story.

E. Define and extend word meaning.

The word *tourist* is used in the story, and it might be a new word for some of the students. Before asking student to complete the reading assignment, write the word on the board. Help the students read the word. Show the students that the word *tour* is in the word, along with a common /ist/ ending sound. Tell students that /ist/ is a suffix that means "someone who does something." A tourist is someone who tours. Ask students to tell about places that they have toured, or have gone to see. A tourist is a person who goes to see new sights.

F. Allow ample time for students to read the story and complete the reading assignment.

Part I: The Reading Connection *(cont.)*

G. Discuss the answers to the reading assignment together.

Answers will vary slightly.

1. *Why does Maxwell want to go on a vacation?* He wants to go on vacation because he wants a break from being neat, he wants time to be by himself, and he wants to see new things.

2. *How will going on vacation help Maxwell?* Going on vacation will help Maxwell because it will give him a break from having to make his bed, it will give him time to read and think, and it will let him see things he's only seen in pictures.

3. *What problems does Maxwell have to solve?* Maxwell has to figure out what to do about missing school. He has to convince his parents to take a vacation. Plus, he has to plan the trip.

4. *What vacation plan does Maxwell tell his parents?* Maxwell tells his parents that he wants to see a waterfall, go on a hike, and then go to a lodge. Then, he wants to go on another hike, have a picnic, and go for a swim. On the last day, he wants to take a drive to see the tourist spots.

5. *How is Maxwell's vacation plan different than his father's vacation plan?* Maxwell plans to go out into the wilderness. Maxwell's father's plan is to go to a big city.

6. Search for patterns the author uses to tell information.

   ✳ Place a funny face (☺) next to the paragraph that compares and contrasts ideas. *(Paragraph 7)*

   ✳ Circle the paragraph that tells ideas in a time order. *(Paragraph 4)*

   ✳ Put a check (✔) next to the two paragraphs that shows cause and effect. *(Paragraphs 2 and 6)*

   ✳ Draw a star (★) next to the paragraph that tells an idea and support. *(Paragraph 1)*

   ✳ Put a question mark (?) next to the paragraph that tells problems and solutions. *(Paragraph 3)*

Part II: The Writing Connection

A. Develop interest in the topic.

Have students generate a list of ways they like to relax. Write the ideas on the board.

watching a movie   flying a kite

going shopping   watching TV

taking a walk   playing soccer

skateboarding   surfing the Web

B. Explain the writing assignment to the students.

Tell the students that they will be designing their own plans to relax. Then, they will write a letter to someone persuading them to join their relaxing plan.

C. Assist students in organizing their writing assignments.

Remind students that newspapers, textbooks, magazines, and stories all have a common ways of presenting information.

* Compare and Contrast   * Idea and Support

* Time Order   * Problem and Solution

* Cause and Effect

Just like good readers learn to look for these patterns as they read, good writers learn to use these patterns to clearly tell information.

Distribute page 69 to students. Lead them through the questions on their writing-assignment handouts. Help students tackle the different writing patterns presented.

D. Allow writing time.

Give students ample time to write their letters. Remind students to use at least three of the patterns of telling information in their letters.

Part II: The Writing Connection *(cont.)*

E. Give students a strategy to help them revise their writing.

Remind students that when people speak, they change the way they speak depending on who they are talking to at the time. For example, when people talk to their bosses at work, they do not speak the same way they do when they are talking to their siblings.

Have students discuss who they use more formal language with (teachers, friends' parents, coaches, aunts and uncles) and who they speak to in a more relaxed language (friends, siblings, cousins, etc.).

Tell students that when they write, their word choice should also change depending on the audience of the writing (i.e., to whom they are writing). Have students think about to whom they are writing their letters and how their wording should change as a result.

F. Give students a strategy to help them edit their writing.

Distribute copies of page 71. Identify the different parts of the friendly letter.

✳ Indent the sender's return address.

✳ Skip a line after the return address, and write the date.

✳ Add the greeting, and follow it with a comma. ("Dear,")

✳ Skip a line, indent, and begin each paragraph.

✳ Indent the closing and follow it with a comma. ("Sincerely," "Yours truly," "Thank you,")

✳ Handwrite a signature.

✳ Print the name of the sender.

Give students time to edit, using the new skill.

G. Publish students' ideas.

Have students select their favorite paragraphs from their letters. The selected paragraph should use one of the patterns of telling information that was discussed in class.

Have students practice reading that paragraph aloud to a partner, then to a small group. Have students focus on reading slowly and loudly. Then have each student read the selected paragraph aloud to the class. Have students identify which pattern each student selected to read.

The Reading Assignment

Directions: Read "Maxwell's Plan" below and on page 68. Students should then answer the questions on page 68.

Maxwell's Plan

Maxwell woke up to the sound of his alarm clock buzzing. It rang for a long time before he even heard it. Suddenly, Max got an idea: he needed to relax. Yes, he needed a vacation. Maxwell was a very neat person, but he was tired of making his bed every day. And although he liked playing with his friends, he needed some time to be by himself. Plus, Maxwell wanted to see something different. "Yes, I really need a vacation," thought Max.

Max knew that if he went on a vacation, he would feel better. He could take a little break from being neat. Then, when he came home, he would be ready to be neat again. Also, if Max could go on vacation, he could take time just for himself. "I could read books, go on walks, and think," thought Max. Then, when he came home, he would be ready to be a good friend again. If Max could get away, he could explore new places. "I would see things I've only seen in pictures," he dreamed. Then, when he came home, he would think about why he liked his home.

Max knew there were some problems with going on vacation. First, he would miss school. Max could solve that problem. "I'll ask my teachers for all the work that I will miss. I can have all of the work finished by the time I get back." Then, Maxwell realized he had to convince his parents that he needed a vacation. Max thought hard about how to solve that problem. He decided that he would show them his excellent report card. Finally, Max knew that his parents did not have time to plan a trip. He realized that he could plan the entire trip so that his parents would not have to do it. Max suddenly got another idea: "I've always wanted to go to a national park. Yes, that is where we should go."

Max spent hours planning his trip. Then, he went to his parents with his plan. "When we get to the park, there are many things we can do and see. First, we can go see a large waterfall. Then, we can go on a hike. After that, let's go to a lodge for dinner. The next day, we can go on another hike. For lunch, I want to have a picnic. Then, we can try to find a place to go swimming. On our last day, I want to drive around and see all the famous tourist spots."

"Hmmm…" said Maxwell's mother. "Hmmm…" said Maxwell's father. "What if we can't go?"

"Well," said Maxwell. "I'll make my bed like I do every other morning. I'll enjoy playing with my friends. Together, we'll go to our favorite neighborhood spots. I'll be okay."

The Reading Assignment *(cont.)*

Maxwell's Plan *(cont.)*

That night, Maxwell's father laughed. He had just started planning a trip to Washington, D.C. He thought about the different trips. Maxwell's idea was to go and explore nature. His idea was to go explore a big city. Both trips would be fun.

The next day, the family headed out to a national park of Maxwell's choice. "A good kid needs a good vacation every now and then," his parents thought. Plus, they decided that they needed a vacation that was already planned.

Answer the following questions:

1. Why did Maxwell want to go on a vacation? _____

   _____

2. How would going on vacation help Maxwell? _____

   _____

   _____

3. What problems did Maxwell have to solve? _____

   _____

4. What vacation plan did Maxwell tell his parents? _____

   _____

   _____

5. How was Maxwell's vacation plan different than his father's vacation plan? _____

   _____

   _____

6. Search for patterns the author uses to tell information. Use the information below to help you.

   ✱ Place a funny face (☺) next to the paragraph that compares and contrasts ideas.

   ✱ Circle the paragraph that tells ideas in a time order.

   ✱ Put a check (✔) next to the paragraph that shows cause and effect.

   ✱ Draw a star (★) next to the paragraph that tells an idea and support.

   ✱ Put a question mark (**?**) next to the paragraph that tells problems and solutions.

The Writing Assignment

Directions: Your assignment will be to write a letter that persuades someone to join you as you relax. Before you begin your letter, organize your ideas below.

Choose Your Ideas

How do you want to relax? _____

_____

To whom are you writing your letter? _____

Organize Your Ideas Using Writing Patterns:

✱ **Idea and Support** (*Tell an idea, and then explain the idea.*)

Why do you need to relax? _____

_____

✱ **Cause and Effect** (*Tell how or why something happened or will happen.*)

How will your plan to relax help you (and the person to whom you are writing)? _____

_____

✱ **Problem and Solution** (*Tell a problem and how to solve it.*)

What problems would you have to solve before relaxing? _____

_____

How would you solve the problems? _____

_____

✱ **Time Order** (*Tell things in the order that they happened or will happen.*)

Tell, in order, how you plan to relax. First, _____

_____

_____

✱ **Compare and Contrast** (*Tell how things are the same and how they are different.*)

What is another way that you could relax? _____

_____

Why is your first plan better than this new plan? _____

_____

The Writing Assignment *(cont.)*

Directions: Write a letter to someone persuading them to join you as you relax. Use at least three different patterns of telling information in your letter. Use "Friendly-Letter Format" on page 71 to help you.

_____

_____

_____

_____

_____

_____

_____

_____

_____

_____

_____

_____

_____

The Writing Assignment *(cont.)*

Friendly-Letter Format

Street Number and Address

City, State and Zip Code

Today's Date

Dear _____,

Skip a line and indent the first paragraph.

Skip a line and indent the next paragraph.

Continue to skip lines and indent each paragraph until you are finished writing your letter.

Sincerely,

Your Signature

Your Printed Name

The Reading Connection

Teacher Directions: Evaluate the answers to the reading assignment.

Objective	Possible Points	Earned Points
You understood the information that you read in a story.		
You found different patterns that the author used to tell information in a story.		
Total Earned Points:		

The Writing Connection

Teacher Directions: Evaluate the letter.

Objective	Possible Points	Earned Points
You wrote about a relaxing plan.		
You told information in at least three different ways.		
You thought about the person you were writing to, and you chose words for that person.		
You set up your letter correctly.		
You put cffort into the writing process.		
Total Earned Points:		

Additional Teacher Comments: _____

_____

_____

_____

Objectives

Reading

✔ To identify personification, alliteration, onomatopoeia, simile, metaphor, imagery, and hyperbole

Writing

✔ To write creatively using personification, alliteration, onomatopoeia, simile, metaphor, imagery, and hyperbole

✔ To select a writing format

✔ To identify when and how to break grammar rules

Lesson Summary

The students will study the following literary devices:

✳ personification   ✳ simile   ✳ imagery

✳ alliteration   ✳ metaphor   ✳ hyperbole

✳ onomatopoeia

The students will identify examples of each in a poem called "A Boat Afloat." Then, the students will complete a creative-writing assignment about an object, using their own examples of the literary devices they have learned. Students will also be introduced to some of the other fun elements of creative writing, such as breaking the rules of grammar and writing in creative formations.

Materials Needed

✳ copies of the reading assignment (pages 77–78)

✳ copies of the writing assignment (page 79)

✳ copies of the "Common Tricks to Writing Creatively" half-sheet (page 74)

Part I: The Reading Connection

A. Develop interest in the topic.

Tell students that they are going to read a poem called "A Boat Afloat." Individually or in small groups, have the students create a list of possible words that might be in a poem about boats. Answers will vary but might include the words *water, seagulls, boat, float, deck,* and *sail.*

B. Encourage students to make predictions about the reading.

Explain to the students that they have already made predictions about words that they might find in the poem. Ask them to make more predictions about the poem, sharing what they know about poetry. *Ask:* "Think about what you know about poems and poetry. What might this poem look like and sound like as you read it?" Allow students to share their knowledge of poetry. Answers might include rhyming words, short sentences, rhythms, etc.

Part I: The Reading Connections *(cont.)*

B. Encourage students to make predictions about the reading. *(cont.)*

Point out that poetry is a way of using words as art. Explain that poetry does not necessarily have rules that must be followed, which is one reason why people find poetry so creative and interesting. For example, most poetry does not have to have rhyming words, punctuation, capital letters, or even be written in straight lines. It is a free form of writing. There are, however, specific types of poems that do follow certain rules.

C. Encourage good reading habits.

Explain that there are some common tricks that authors use when they write creatively. Understanding these common creative tricks makes reading more fun and easier to understand.

Copy, cut out, and distribute copies of the half-sheet below. Teach students the common tricks of writing creatively that authors can use. Have students write examples on the blank lines as you discuss them in class. Answers may vary, but examples are provided.

Common Tricks to Writing Creatively

Personification is *making something that is not alive act like a human.*
* ✳ The comb's teeth bit into my scalp.

Alliteration is *using the same sounds several times.*
* ✳ Through the window, we were watching Will work in the wind.

Onomatopoeia are *words that are an imitation of a sound.*
* ✳ Splat!

Metaphor is *a comparison.*
* ✳ She is a flower petal, quiet and delicate.

Simile is *a type of metaphor that uses the words "like" or "as."*
* ✳ She is as loud as a tuba.

Imagery is *the use of words that tell what something looks like, smells like, feels like, sounds like, or tastes like.*
* ✳ The new, red Mustang was so shiny that I could see my reflection on it.

Hyperbole is *exaggeration.*
* ✳ I have so much homework that it will take me a week to complete it all.

Part I: The Reading Connections *(cont.)*

D. Establish a purpose for reading.

Pass out copies of "A Boat Afloat" (page 77) for the students to read. Have students find an example of personification, alliteration, onomatopoeia, simile, metaphor, imagery, and hyperbole within the poem.

E. Define and extend word meaning.

The word *afloat* is used in the story, and it might be a new word for some of the students.

Have students examine the word to find a smaller, more familiar word in the word *afloat*. The students should recognize the word *float*. Tell students that the word *afloat* means "floating." (*Example:* The ducks were afloat on the lake.)

F. Allow ample time for students to read the story and complete the reading assignment.

Hand out page 78. Depending on the classroom situation, you might want to have the students complete this in small groups.

G. Discuss the answers to the reading assignment together.

Answers may vary, but the following are acceptable responses:

Personification: sails waving, lights beaming, ropes cheering, kitchen squealing, and deck gleaming

Alliteration: sliding through spaces as small as soap bars

Onomatopoeia: water gushing, bells clanging, insects buzzing, cabin doors banging, fishing rods clicking, wet clothes dripping, paddles splashing, waves smashing

Simile: rolling in water as clear as glass, bowing through water like a great bass

Metaphor: the anchor, heavier than treasure

Imagery: deck gleaming, wheel spinning, crew dreaming, captain steaming

Hyperbole: spaces as small as soap bars, masts reaching as high as the stars

Part II: The Writing Connection

A. Develop interest in the topic.

With the students' help, create a list of objects (e.g., chair, toothbrush, rainbow, computer) on the board. Have each student pick an object. As an alternative, you can do the writing assignment as a class (using one object) or in small groups (using selected or assigned objects).

Part II: The Writing Connection *(cont.)*

B. Explain the writing assignment to the students.

Explain that they are going to do some creative writing about their objects, using some common creative-writing tricks that authors use. (Explain that they won't be expected to write a poem like the reading selection in the other part of the lesson.) If you haven't already, guide your students through "Common Tricks to Writing Creatively" (page 74).

C. Assist students in organizing their creative-writing assignment.

Help the students gather their ideas. Guide the students through the writing-assignment handout (page 79).

D. Allow writing time.

Have students begin to put their creative writing ideas together. Move on to **Step E** rather quickly, though. (**Step E** will give the students an idea of the different formats they can use when writing creatively.)

E. Give students a strategy to help them revise their writing.

Explain to the students that what they write is important, but how they choose to present the information is important, as well. Tell the students that people write in many different formats. People can write friendly letters, business letters, news articles, advertisements, reports, lists, paragraphs, etc. Creative writing can take on any of these formats and more. Creative writing can be done in straight lines or curves, and the writing can even take the form of an object, like the object they are describing.

Have students select a format to use. Allow students to select a simple paragraph or a more creative format. Give students more time to write, using their selected formats.

F. Give students a strategy to help them edit their writing.

Teach students that when writing creatively, they do not need to use all of the rules of the English language that they usually use. However, rules should be broken the same way throughout the writing. For example, if students choose not to use capital letters or complete sentences, they should continue to "break the rule" throughout the entire piece of writing. Encourage students to also think about why they might want to break a rule and how it might make their writing more interesting. For example, if students are writing about a dictionary, they might choose to misspell words for humor, since a job of a dictionary is to provide correct spelling. Give students time to edit their papers.

G. Publish students' ideas.

Option 1: Create a booklet with all the students' writing. Give each student a copy of the booklet to keep.

Option 2: Have students select a part of their writing that uses one of the creative-writing tricks. Have them read the selection aloud and have the class identify which creative-writing trick was being used.

The Reading Assignment

Directions: Read "A Boat Afloat" below. As you read, look for examples of the following literary tricks:

* **Personification**   * **Simile**   * **Imagery**
* **Alliteration**   * **Metaphor**   * **Hyperbole**
* **Onomatopoeia**

A Boat Afloat

floating in the fishes' home   water gushing, bells clanging

docking where the dolphins dome   insects buzzing, cabin doors banging

rolling in water as clear as glass   fishing rods clicking, wet clothes dripping

bowing through water like a great bass   paddles splashing, waves smashing

sails waving, lights beaming   sliding through spaces as small as soap bars

ropes cheering, kitchen squealing   with masts reaching as high as the stars

deck gleaming, wheel spinning   the anchor, heavier than treasure

crew dreaming, captain steaming   afloat for work, afloat for pleasure

The Reading Assignment *(cont.)*

Directions: Writers use many literary tricks to make their creations more interesting. Below are some of those tricks. Fill in examples of each from the poem "A Boat Afloat."

Personification—making something that is not alive act like a human

Example(s) from "A Boat Afloat": _____

_____

Alliteration—using the same sounds several times

Example(s) from "A Boat Afloat": _____

_____

Onomatopoeia—words that are imitations of sounds

Example(s) from "A Boat Afloat": _____

_____

Metaphor—a comparison (*Note:* Don't use the words "like" or "as")

Example(s) from "A Boat Afloat": _____

_____

Simile—a type of metaphor that uses the words "like" or "as"

Example(s) from "A Boat Afloat": _____

_____

Imagery—words that tell what something looks like, smells like, feels like, sounds like, or tastes like.

Example(s) from "A Boat Afloat": _____

_____

Hyperbole—an exaggeration

Example(s) from "A Boat Afloat": _____

_____

Lesson
Nine

The Writing Assignment

Directions: Write about an object of your choice, using creative tricks that authors use.

What is your object? _____

Use Creative Writing Tricks

✳ Give your object some human traits. (*Personification*) _____

_____

✳ Repeat a sound when writing part of the description. (*Alliteration*) _____

_____

✳ Have your object make a sound. (*Onomatopoeia*)_____

_____

✳ Compare your object to something else by saying that your object is the other item. (*Metaphor*)

_____

_____

✳ Compare your object to something else, using the word "like" or "as." (*Simile*) _____

_____

✳ Exaggerate something that your object can do. (*Hyperbole*)_____

_____

✳ Appeal to your readers' senses. (*Imagery*)

 1. Describe what your objects looks like: _____

_____

 2. Describe sounds that your object can make: _____

_____

 3. Describe what your object might smell like: _____

_____

 4. Describe what your object can taste like: _____

_____

 5. Describe what your object might feel like: _____

_____

The Reading Connection

Teacher Directions: Evaluate the answers to the reading assignment.

Objective	Possible Points	Earned Points
You found examples of personification, alliteration, onomatopoeia, simile, metaphor, imagery, and hyperbole in a poem.		
Total Earned Points:		

The Writing Connection

Teacher Directions: Evaluate the creative writing.

Objective	Possible Points	Earned Points
You used personification, alliteration, onomatopoeia, simile, metaphor, imagery, and hyperbole.		
Format: You chose how to write your description.		
You used (or broke!) rules the same way all through your creative writing.		
You put effort into the writing process.		
Total Earned Points:		

Additional Teacher Comments: _____

_____

_____

_____

_____

Objectives

Reading

✔ To understand the differences between main characters and minor characters

✔ To identify how and why characters change

✔ To identify and evaluate important actions of characters

✔ To understand how appearance affects other characters and the reader

✔ To relate to characters personally

✔ To make predictions

Writing

✔ To write a fully developed character description

✔ To brainstorm ideas using real and fictional ideas

✔ To evaluate ideas

✔ To organize ideas into similar groups

✔ To use dialogue

✔ To use commas when listing items in a series and when separating ideas

Lesson Summary

The students will read a story called "Sam the Snake." Then, the students will write an original, fully-developed character description.

Materials Needed

✱ copies of the reading assignment (pages 86–88).

✱ copies of the writing assignment (pages 89–90).

✱ handout or overhead of "Understanding Characters" (page 88).

Part I: The Reading Connection

A. Develop interest in the topic.

Have students discuss some interesting characters that they have read about or seen in the movies or television.

B. Encourage students to make predictions about the reading.

Tell the students that they will be reading a story called "Sam the Snake." Ask students to make predictions about the story. *Ask:* "Based on the title of the story, what do you think this story might be about?" Allow students to give creative answers. Encourage students to make predictions about the type of character Sam the Snake might be.

Part I:　The Reading Connection *(cont.)*

C.　Encourage good reading habits.

Remind students that stories have characters. Some characters are described in great detail; others are described in less detail. Readers need to be able to recognize the important characters in a story so that the reader can focus on them.

Hand out and review "Understanding Characters" (page 88) with the students.

D.　Establish a purpose for reading.

Pass out copies of "Sam the Snake" for the students to read. Encourage students to focus on the characters in the story. Read aloud the questions that the students should answer as they read the story.

E.　Define and extend word meaning.

The word *loner* is used in the story, and it might be a new word for some of the students.

Ask the students what words they know that are similar to the word loner. Students might be able to identify the words *alone* or *lonely*. Explain that a loner is a person who likes to be alone.

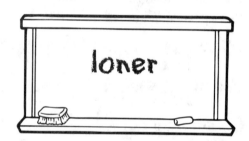

F.　Allow ample time for students to read the story and complete the reading assignment.

G.　Discuss the answers to the reading assignment.

1. *Who are the two main characters in the story?* Sam the Snake and Tommy are the two main characters in the story.

2. *Who are the two minor characters in the story?* Tommy's mother and Sheriff Boots are the two minor characters in the story.

3. *How does the author develop one of the main characters?* Students may choose to describe Tommy or Sam the Snake. Sam wears snakeskin boots, a buckle with a picture of a snake, is respected by people, speaks with a snake-like hiss, and is a loner. Tommy is eight or nine, goes unnoticed much of the time, likes the respect Sam gets, and has a mother who is busy working.

4. *How does the author describe one of the minor characters?* Students may choose to describe Sheriff Boots or Tommy's mother. Sheriff Boots is a typical Western sheriff, wears boots with heals that click, has sagging pants, and speaks slowly. Tommy's mother is tired because she works very hard. She is a single, hardworking mother.

Part I: The Reading Connection *(cont.)*

G. Discuss the answers to the reading assignment. *(cont.)*

5. *How might Sam's look affect the way other characters and the reader react to him?* Sam's appearance might remind people of snakes, which can be dangerous. That might make people afraid of him.

6. *In your opinion, what is the most important thing that one of the characters does in the story?* Answers will vary. For example, it is important that Tommy chooses to search for Sam the Snake. That decision changes both of their lives.

7. *Why do you think Tommy and Sam get along so well?* Answers might vary. Tommy and Sam are both alone much of the time. People are a little afraid of Sam, and people do not notice Tommy.

8. *Think about a character that changes in the story. How and why does that character change?* Answers will vary. For example, one character that changes in the story is Sam the Snake. After talking to Tommy, he learns that people want to become his friend.

9. *Think about one thing that a character does in the story. Tell why you would or would not have done the same thing.* Answers will vary.

10. *Tell why you are like or unlike one of the characters in the story.* Answers will vary.

11. *Think about one more thing that a character could have said in the story or after the story ended. What would the character have said, and why?* Answers will vary.

Part II: The Writing Connection

A. Develop interest in the topic.

Distribute page 89 to students and have them complete "Step One: List Your Ideas" on the writing-assignment handout. You might want to explain to students that writers get ideas by looking at what they know. Once the ideas start coming, then fictional writers start making their writing interesting by adding fictional, or untrue, details. You can point out to the students that their characters are going to be fictional. Encourage them to add interesting details to their lists, even if they are not true.

B. Explain the writing assignment to the students.

Explain to the students that they are going to create a fully-developed character. That means they are going to describe a character that they create in as much detail as possible. The more details that the students are able to provide, the better other people will be able to picture their character.

Part I: The Reading Connection *(cont.)*

C. Assist students in organizing their character descriptions.

Hand out page 90 and guide students through "Step Two: Pick Your Best Ideas" and "Step Three: Organize Your Ideas" of their writing assignment. Encourage students to add as many details onto their lists as possible. Once again, you might want to remind students that their details don't have to be true, but they should be interesting.

D. Allow writing time.

Once students have grouped their ideas, have students begin putting their ideas into paragraphs. A writing method students can use is to put each organized group of ideas from Step Three into a separate paragraph.

Give students ample time to write their paragraphs. As they are working, walk around the room and offer guidance.

E. Give students a strategy to help them revise their writing.

Explain to the students that one way to make their character fully developed is to give the character a voice, called "dialogue." Have the students think about something that their character might say, and how the character might sound saying it. Then, have them put the dialogue into their character descriptions.

F. Give students a strategy to help them edit their writing.

Remind students to use commas when separating ideas or when listing things. Write the following example on the board.

✸ *My character has freckles, curly hair, and blue-green eyes.*

Show students how commas are used in the example to separate the descriptions. Have students check to make sure they did this correctly in their writing. If students do not have any similar sentences in their writing, tell students to add at least one into their writing to show that they can use the skill correctly.

Give students time to edit, using the new skill.

G. Publish students' ideas.

Option 1: Collect and randomly redistribute the students' character descriptions, making sure that no student gets the description he/she wrote. Have students read their assigned descriptions and draw a sketch of the character.

Option 2: Hang pictures around the room. Have each student pick the sketch that they think matches the character they created. Have students discuss why they drew what they did and have authors discuss how they knew which drawing was their character.

The Reading Assignment

Directions: Read "Sam the Snake" below and on page 86. Answer the questions on page 87.

Sam the Snake

Sam the Snake. That is what everyone called him in the small town of Homestead. Sam the Snake. They called him that for a few reasons. First, he wore a great big silver belt buckle with a picture of a snake on it. He also wore cowboy boots made out of snake skin. Plus, when he talked, he sounded like a snake.

"Hey there, boysssssss," he'd say. "Howsssss it going?"

There were rumors that there were even snakes living on his ranch, but no one knew for sure. Sam the Snake was a loner. He was the type of person that you wanted to know but were afraid to know—all at the same time.

One day, Sam the Snake disappeared. No one knew where he was. The people in the town went to Sheriff Boots to ask what they should do. Sheriff Boots walked across the front porch, the black heels of his boots clicking on the wood. He hiked up his pants, cleared his throat, and slowly spoke.

"Well, Sam the Snake is a grown man. He can come and go as he pleases. Unless you have proof that something is wrong, I can't help you."

There was a little boy in town that no one paid much attention to, unless he got into trouble. His name was Tommy. He was about eight or nine years old. His mother worked several jobs. She did her best to take care of Tommy, but she was so busy and so tired that she did not have the energy to raise him properly.

Tommy liked Sam the Snake. He liked the way he slithered into the town. He liked the respect that people showed him. He liked the way that Sam showed respect to other people, as well. He would hold doors open for people, tip his hat, say "please" and "thank you," and help people who needed help if he saw the need.

Tommy was upset that Sam the Snake was missing. He felt that something was wrong. He knew he was only a boy, but he believed that he had to do whatever he could to find out if Sam was in trouble.

He decided to check out Sam the Snake's ranch first. He was a little scared to enter the house. He, too, had heard the rumors of the snakes. But he felt it was the right thing to do.

The Reading Assignment *(cont.)*

Sam the Snake *(cont.)*

He entered through a small window. There were no live snakes that he could see. What he did find was that everything was in its place. In fact, it looked like Sam had planned to be gone for awhile.

Then, Tommy noticed that Sam's snakeskin boots were there. And his belt buckle was there, too.

Tommy panicked. He started to run. He ran towards the big city that was far away. Maybe the sheriff of the big city would help him. After awhile, he began to wish he brought his bike, and some water. But, he had to keep going. All of a sudden, his legs gave out. He fell to the ground, exhausted, and crying.

"What'ssssss wrong, Thomassssssssss?" he heard.

Tommy gasped. "You know my name?" he asked.

"Of courssssssssse," said Sam the Snake. "Where are you going?"

"I was looking for you!"

"Me?" asked Sam the Snake. "Why? No one ever looksss for me."

"I was worried about you. We were all worried about you. Where were you?'

"I was lonely," said Sam the Snake. "I went to the big cccity to sssee if I could meet sssomeone ssspecial. But the big cccity is too big for me. I like it better back in Homessstead, even if I am lonely."

"Lonely?" questioned Tommy. "You? Do you know how many people would like to be your friend in our town?" Then there was a thoughtful pause. "Why did you leave your boots at home? And your buckle?" asked Tommy.

"I thought it might ssscare away the ladiesss," sighed Sam the Snake.

That night, and on many nights to come, Sam the Snake ate dinner with Tommy and his mother. And soon, Tommy's mother started wearing dresses in snakeskin prints, and Tommy started wearing snakeskin boots that were just his size.

And that is how a small boy who no one paid attention to changed the lives of many people. And that is how the town learned that everyone, even a person like Sam the Snake, needed a friend.

The Reading Assignment *(cont.)*

Answer the following questions about "Sam the Snake":

1. Who are the two main characters in the story? _____

    _____

2. Who are the two minor characters in the story? _____

    _____

3. How does the author develop one of the main characters? _____

    _____

4. How does the author describe one of the minor characters? _____

    _____

5. How might Sam's look affect the way other characters and the reader react to him? _____

    _____

6. In your opinion, what is the most important thing that one of the characters does in the story?

    _____

    _____

7. Why do you think Tommy and Sam get along so well? _____

    _____

8. Think about a character that changes in the story. How and why does that character change?

    _____

    _____

9. Think about one thing that a character does in the story. Tell why you would or would not have done the same thing. _____

    _____

10. Tell why you are like or unlike one of the characters in the story. _____

    _____

11. Think about one more thing that a character could have said in the story or after the story ended. What would the character have said and why? _____

    _____

Understanding Characters

Main Characters

    ✳ described with many details

    ✳ important to the story

Minor Characters

    ✳ often given common descriptions

    ✳ less important to the story

Once a reader knows that a character is important, the reader can spend time "getting to know" the character by doing the following:

    ✳ creating images of the character in his/her head

    ✳ slowing down when reading descriptions of that character

    ✳ carefully looking at things that the character says and does

    ✳ thinking about why the character says and does certain things

    ✳ thinking about what the character should and should not do

    ✳ thinking about how and why characters change

    ✳ thinking about what you would do if you were in the story

    ✳ thinking about how you are like or unlike the character

Minor characters are put in a story to interact with the main characters.

Lesson
Ten

The Writing Assignment

Directions: Create a fully-developed character.

☛ **Step One: List Your Idea**

Describe yourself. What do you look like? What do you sound like? How do others see you?
What are you like? What do you like to do?

_____   _____

_____   _____

_____   _____

Think about an adult that you know. What does this person look like? What does the person sound
like? What is the person like? What does this person like to do?

_____   _____

_____   _____

_____   _____

Think about a person in the media. What does this person look like? What does the person sound
like? What is the person like?

_____   _____

_____   _____

_____   _____

List other interesting descriptions that you can think of in people that you know. What interesting
looks do people you know have? What interesting personalities do people you know have? What
interesting things do people you know do?

_____   _____

_____   _____

_____   _____

The Writing Assignment *(cont.)*

☞ **Step Two: Pick Your Best Ideas**

Look over your list. Circle the most interesting details. Use the ideas to help you create your own new, interesting character. If you think of other ideas, write them down, too.

_____   _____

_____   _____

_____   _____

_____   _____

☞ **Step Three: Organize Your Ideas**

Group your similar ideas. Write down the following:

Details that describe what your character looks like:

_____   _____

Details that describe what your character sounds like:

_____   _____

_____   _____

Details that describe what your character's personality is like:

_____   _____

Details that describe how others see your character:

_____   _____

Details that describe what your character does:

_____   _____

Other important details:

_____   _____

_____   _____

The Reading Connection

Teacher Directions: Evaluate the answers to the reading questions.

Objective	Possible Points	Earned Points
You identified major and minor characters.		
You identified how and why a character changes.		
You identified and evaluated a character's actions.		
You understand the importance of character descriptions.		
You relate to the characters personally.		
You can make predictions about what characters might say.		
Total Earned Points:		

The Writing Connection

Teacher Directions: Evaluate the character descriptions.

Objective	Possible Points	Earned Points
Your character was fully developed.		
You organized your ideas.		
You used dialogue.		
You used commas when listing items in a series or separating ideas.		
You put effort into using the writing process.		
Total Earned Points:		

Additional Teacher Comments: _____

_____

Objectives

Reading

✔ To identify the five parts of a story's plot: introduction, rising action, climax, falling action, and conclusion

Writing

✔ To write the falling action and conclusion to a given story

✔ To add details to a story as a revision strategy

✔ To use capital letters correctly

Lesson Summary

The students will read a story called "The Shoe Switch" and identify different parts of the story's plot. Then, students will write the ending of a story called "Fair Game."

Materials Needed

✴ copies of the reading assignment (pages 95–96)

✴ copies of the writing assignment (page 97)

Part I: The Reading Connection

A. Develop interest in the topic.

Ask: "If you could switch places with someone just for a day, who would you switch places with, and why?" Allow students to respond.

B. Encourage students to make predictions about the reading.

Tell the students that they will be reading a story called "The Shoe Switch." Ask students to make predictions about the story. *Ask:* "Based on the title of the story, what do you think this story might be about?" Allow students to give creative answers.

C. Encourage good reading habits.

Tell students that plot is the movement of a story from the beginning to the end. There are five basic parts of a story's plot. Depending on the level of the students, you may or may not want to focus on the technical terms of all five parts of the plot. (**Note:** You may wish to display on an overhead the "Five Basic Parts of a Plot" box on page 93.)

Explain that understanding how a story is told helps readers follow along as they are reading. Point out that not all stories have all five of the plot parts covered in this lesson.

Part I: The Reading Connection *(cont.)*

Five Basic Parts of a Plot

1. **Introduction:** Readers are told who the story is about and when and where the story takes place.

2. **Rising Action:** The problem is told.

3. **Climax:** Something happens to stop the problem from growing bigger.

4. **Falling Action:** The problem begins to reach an end.

5. **Conclusion:** The problem is ended.

D. Establish a purpose for reading.

Distribute copies of "The Shoe Switch" (pages 95 and 96) to students. Tell the students that as they read they should look for the five different parts of the plot. Read aloud the instructions that are on the handout.

E. Define and extend word meaning.

The word *client* appears in the story, and it might be a new word for the students. Explain to the students that a client is a person who gets help from a professional worker.

client

F. Allow ample time for students to read the story and complete the reading assignment.

G. Discuss the answers to the reading assignment together.

1. The introduction of this story is located in the first paragraph.

2. The rising action in this story is the problem between the twins. Each girl thinks that her job is the most important, and they argue every time they see each other.

3. The climax is when the man suggests to the twins that they switch places with each other.

4. The falling action of the story is when each person realizes that the other person has a hard, important job, as well.

5. The conclusion is that each twin learns to be proud of her sister's hard, important job.

Part II: The Writing Connection

A. Develop interest in the topic.

Ask: "Have you ever seen a game get out of control?" Allow students time to share their experiences.

B. Explain the writing assignment to the students.

Tell the students that they will be reading part of a story about a game that gets out of control. There is a referee in the story. The job of the referee is to make sure that the game is played fairly. So, the referee has a plan to fix the problem.

Tell the students that the story has no ending. The students will write the falling action and the conclusion of the story. Remind the students that the falling action is the part of the story where the problem tries to get fixed. The conclusion is the ending of the story, and it tells us if the problem does get fixed.

C. Assist students in organizing their ideas.

1. Distribute copies of "Fair Game" (page 97) and give students time to read the material.

2. Put students in small groups to discuss possible endings to the story.

3. Regroup as a class. Have students share some of their ideas as you jot down an idea list on the board.

D. Allow writing time.

Give students ample time to write their own endings to the story. As they are working, walk around the room offering guidance.

E. Give students a strategy to help them revise their writing.

Tell students that details are what make stories interesting. Encourage the students to go back to the original story and add details, like names of teams, the places where the teams were from, a name for the referee, a description of the type of sport being played, etc. Not only will this make the story more interesting, but it will make the story more original.

F. Give students a strategy to help them edit their writing.

Remind students that names are capitalized. Names of people, places, and teams are also capitalized. Names of general sports, however, are not capitalized. But if the game has a special name, like the Super Bowl, then it is capitalized. Have the students check to see that they used correct capitalization in their stories.

G. Publish students' ideas.

Option 1: Select some particularly unique versions of the story to read aloud to the class.

Option 2: Have student select their favorite parts of their stories to share with the class.

Lesson Eleven

The Reading Assignment

Directions: Read "The Shoe Switch" below and on page 96. Follow the instructions on page 96.

The Shoe Switch

Mary and Marcie were twins. Mary was a teacher at the elementary school near her home. Marcie was a lawyer not far away. Every time Mary and Marcie got together, they argued about whose job was harder.

Marcie would say, "My job is so hard. I have to learn so many different laws! There are so many cases that I need to work on at once. There are so many clients that I need to help. And I have to work late at night to be ready for the next day. My job affects people's lives."

Then, Marci would say, "Oh, your job is hard? You talk about your cases over fancy meals. You have people to help you with your job.

My job affect's people's lives, too. Every day, I need to be prepared to teach many children. They count on me to teach them and to answer their questions. I need to help them when they are sad, and to take care of them when they are hurt. I have to give them advice when they are confused and help them to make good decisions. Then when I go home, I have to grade papers and make a new lesson for the next day. My job is harder than yours."

Every time the twins got together, they would have the same argument. One day, a wise old man overheard them. "Wear each other's shoes" was the only thing he said to them.

At first, the twins were confused. How would switching shoes help to end the argument? But, they switched shoes, anyway. "Your shoes are so uncomfortable," said Marcie to Mary. Then Mary said, "I think that the wise old man meant for us to switch more than just our shoes." "You are right," said Marcie. "Let's switch places." And so they did.

The Reading Assignment *(cont.)*

The Shoe Switch *(cont.)*

Mary was tired by the end of the day. Her head was filled with laws she did not understand. She met so many people and could not remember what anyone had said to her. She realized that her sister did have a job that was harder than hers.

Marcie was tired by the end of the day, as well. She realized that there were so many young children who had really needed her. She realized that her sister did have a job that was harder than hers.

"You're right," the twins said at the same time when they saw each other.

"Actually, we are both wrong," said Marcie. "We should have understood that each of us had important and hard jobs. I'm proud of what you do."

"I'm proud of you, too," said Mary. "Now, can I have my shoes back?"

As you read the story, do the following:

1. **Circle the *introduction*.**

   The *introduction* tells who the story is about and when and where the story takes place.

2. **Put a question mark (?) near the *rising action*.**

   The *rising action* is the growing problem in the story.

3. **Put an exclamation mark (!) near the *climax*.**

   At the *climax*, something happens to stop the problem from growing bigger.

4. **Put a down arrow (↓) near the *falling action*.**

   During the *falling action*, the problem begins to come to an end.

5. **Draw a smiley face (☺) at the *conclusion*.**

   In the *conclusion*, the problem ends.

Lesson Eleven

The Writing Assignment

Directions: Finish the story by adding the falling action and the conclusion.

Fair Game

Two teams walked onto the field. It was cold and rainy, but the teams were ready to play. This was the last game of the season. Both teams wanted to win. But the referee was worried. The teams played unfairly before.

During the past, players distracted the referee so that someone could cheat. Players said hurtful things to the other team, in order to make them upset. The referee thought about ending the game. But then the referee came up with a better plan.

The referee blew the whistle. The two teams listened to what the referee had to say. The referee said that five players from each team would have to switch teams. "This will help to make the game fair," explained the referee.

What happens next? (*This is the falling action of the story. How does the referee's idea affect the problem in the story?*)

_____

_____

_____

_____

_____

How does the story end? (*This is the conclusion. How is the problem solved?*)

_____

_____

_____

_____

_____

The Reading Connection

Teacher Directions: Evaluate the reading assignment.

Objective	Possible Points	Earned Points
You found the different parts of the story's plot.		
Total Earned Points:		

The Writing Connection

Teacher Directions: Evaluate the story.

Objective	Possible Points	Earned Points
You wrote the falling action for your story.		
You wrote an ending for your story.		
You added details into your story.		
You capitalized words correctly.		
You put effort into the writing process.		
Total Earned Points:		

Additional Teacher Comments: _____

_____

_____

_____

_____

Objectives

Reading

- ✔ To identify the purpose of reading textbooks, types of textbooks, and who uses textbooks

- ✔ To identify different parts of a textbooks

- ✔ To identify how textbooks are organized

Writing

- ✔ To write paragraphs using compare/contrast, problem/solution, idea/support, cause/effect, and time-order patterns

- ✔ To use words specific to a topic

- ✔ To spell uncommon words correctly

Lesson Summary

The students will read a sample chapter of a textbook called *All About Learning.* Then, the students will write paragraphs, using common patterns that textbooks use to tell information.

Materials Needed

- ✳ copies of the reading assignment (pages 103–105)

- ✳ copies of the writing assignment (pages 106–105)

- ✳ a variety of textbooks (*optional*)

- ✳ dictionaries

Part I: The Reading Connection

A. Develop interest in the topic.

Ask the following questions:

1. "How many textbooks do you have?" Answers will vary.

2. "What kinds of textbooks do you have?" Answers will vary.

3. "What kinds of textbooks do you NOT have, but other people might have?" Answers will vary but might include medical or law textbooks.

4. "How is a textbook different from other types of books?" Answers will vary according to students' knowledge of textbooks. Encourage students to tell you anything they know about textbooks.

Part I: The Reading Connection *(cont.)*

B. Encourage students to make predictions about the reading.

Tell the students that they will be reading a chapter from a textbook. The title of the chapter that they will read is called "Learning About Textbooks."

Ask: "What might you read about in the chapter called 'Learning About Textbooks?'" Students' answers will vary.

C. Encourage good reading habits.

Remind students that textbooks are hard to read because many new words are used in textbooks. Every subject has special words, and those words have to be used when talking about the subject.

Discuss with students some hard words that they might find in different textbooks. For example, a music textbook will have words such as *treble, clef,* and *harmony.* Science textbooks will have words such as *molecules* and *dissection.* Geography books might have names of new places.

Tell students that they might see some hard words to read in this chapter. Write the following terms on the board: *table of contents, index, glossary, units, chapters, headings, italics,* and *textbook.* Give students time to become comfortable reading and saying these words.

D. Establish a purpose for reading.

Hand out pages 103–105 to students. Tell students that the purpose of reading this chapter is to learn about textbooks. Instruct students to complete the chart as they read the chapter and to answer the questions that are given.

E. Define and extend word meaning.

Explain that there might be many new words in the chapter, such as *index* and *glossary.* Students should try to use the information provided in the chapter to learn the definition of these words. Explain that textbooks often use hard words, but definitions for those words are usually provided.

F. Allow ample time for students to read the story and complete the reading assignment.

Part I: The Reading Connection *(cont.)*

G. Discuss the answers to the reading assignment together.

	What is it?	When do you use it?	How is it organized?	Where is it?
Table of Contents	a list of all the units and chapters	when you need to find a page number for a unit or chapter	in the order that the units and chapters are written	in the front of the book
Index	a list of ideas that are taught in the book	when you want to find the page where the idea is explained	in A–Z order	at the end of the book
Glossary	a list of hard words, and their definitions	when you want to learn the definition of a word	in A–Z order	at the end of the book
Heading	words that tell the reader what the sentences under it are about	to help you find information easily	large words that are on top of the sentences	in the chapters

1. *What did you already know before reading this chapter about textbooks?* Answers will vary.

2. *What did you learn from reading this chapter about textbooks?* Answers will vary.

3. *What could Chapter Two of* All About Learning *be called?* Answers will vary, but should relate to textbooks. Answers might include "How Textbooks are Made," "How to Write a Textbook," "How to Read a Textbook," etc.

4. *What could Unit Two of* All About Learning *be called?* Answers will vary, but should relate to learning. Answers might include, "All About Teachers," "All About Schools," "All About Classes," etc.

5. *What pictures could be found in "Chapter One: All About Textbooks"?* Answers will vary, but might include, "pictures of different textbooks, pictures of a table of contents, pictures of an index, etc."

6. *How are textbooks different from other books?* Answers will vary. For example, textbooks have units, glossaries, and an index. Most books do not. Also, the purpose of a textbook is to teach information about a particular subject.

H. Show samples

Show students some different examples of textbooks, if you have them available. Point out the different sections that can be found in the textbooks.

Part II: The Writing Connection

A. Develop interest in the topic.

Have students create a list of as many possible textbook topics that they can. List many of their examples on the board. For example, math, science, art, sports, cooking, car mechanics, computer security, Lego design, pet care, hobbies, etc.

B. Explain the writing assignment to the students.

Explain to the students that information in textbooks is written in common ways. It is common for textbooks to tell information using these following patterns:

* ✳ compare and contrast
* ✳ time order
* ✳ cause and effect
* ✳ idea and support
* ✳ problem and solution

Today, they will be looking at these different ways that textbooks tell information. They will also be reading examples of these different ways of telling information.

Hand out pages 106–107. Tell the students that they will be writing paragraphs using the different ways to tell information. (*Have students select any three to complete.*)

(**Note:** If you think your students need more practice working with these structural patterns, you might want to review "Lesson Eight: Organizational Patterns" on pages 62–72.)

C. Allow writing time.

Give students ample time to write their paragraphs. As they are working, walk around the room and offer guidance.

D. Give students a strategy to help them revise their writing.

Remind students that when writing about a specific topic, there are often words that go along with that topic. For example, if you were writing about surfboards, you might include the words *fins, leashes, deck grips, surfboard wax, wet suits,* and *rash guards*. Have students think about words that are specific to their selected topics.

E. Give students a strategy to help them edit their writing.

Remind students that words that they don't use often are sometimes hard to spell. Encourage students to locate words they are not sure how to spell and to use a dictionary or other source to locate the correct spelling of those words. Give students time to edit.

F. Publish students' ideas.

Have students tear a piece of paper up into five strips. Have them label each paper: *Compare and Contrast, Time Order, Cause and Effect, Idea and Support,* and *Problem and Solution*. Read some of the students' paragraphs aloud. Have the students hold up the strip of paper that they feel best describes how the paragraph was written.

The Reading Assignment

Directions: Read the entry below from the first chapter of the textbook *All About Learning*. Answer the questions at the bottom of page 104 and fill in the chart on page 105.

Unit: All About Textbooks

Chapter One: Learning About Textbooks

1.1 What Textbooks Are

Textbooks are books that teach you about different things. There are many kinds of textbooks. There are science, history, English, language, math, art, music, sewing, woodworking, medical, law, and computer textbooks. There are many more kinds of textbooks, too.

1.2 Textbook Readers

Many people read textbooks. Children and adults all over the world read them. They are used in elementary schools, middle schools, high schools, colleges, and in most classes that are taught. Textbooks can be found in libraries and bookstores. Anyone who wants to learn about something can use a textbook.

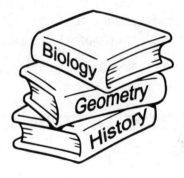

1.3 The Set-Up

Textbooks are set up in special ways. Most textbooks are separated into *units* and *chapters*. *Units* are the big ideas that can be separated into smaller ideas. *Chapters* are the smaller ideas. Sometimes, chapters are separated into even smaller parts. The chapter you are reading now is separated into numbered parts.

Textbooks try to make it easy for people to **find** and **understand** new things.

To help people find information, textbooks have special pages. One special page is called a **table of contents**. The table of contents lists all the units and chapters in order. It tells the pages where the units and chapters are. It is found in the front of the book.

The Reading Assignment *(cont.)*

1.3 The Set-Up *(cont.)*

The **index** lists ideas that can be found in the book. It lists the page numbers where the ideas can be found. Its ideas are listed in alphabetical (A–Z) order. The index is found at the end of the book.

The **glossary** is a dictionary. It defines hard words that are used in the book. It is listed in A–Z order. It is found at the back of the book, too.

To help people understand textbooks, several things are done. Textbooks make words look different. This helps you know which words are important. In the chapter you are reading now, you can see words that are in bold and in italics.

Many textbooks even make some of the words different sizes. These larger words are usually headings. Headings tell the reader about the sentences that are under it. The headings are made large so that your eyes can easily find it on a page. Headings can be found in a chapter. There are three headings in this chapter.

Textbook often include pictures or other kinds of drawing to help you to understand new ideas.

Answer the following questions:

1. What did you already know before reading this chapter about textbooks? _____

   _____

2. What did you learn from reading this chapter about textbooks? _____

   _____

3. What could Chapter Two of *All About Learning* be called? _____

   _____

4. What could Unit Two of *All About Learning* be called?_____

   _____

5. What pictures might be found in "Chapter One: Learning About Textbooks"? _____

   _____

6. How are textbooks different from other books? _____

   _____

The Reading Assignment *(cont.)*

Directions: After reading the information from Chapter One of *All About Learning*, fill in this chart.

	What is it?	When do you use it?	How is it organized?	Where is it?
Table of Contents				
Index				
Glossary				
Heading				

The Writing Assignment

Directions: Write paragraphs using the different ways to tell information. Select any three on this page and page 107.

1. **Compare and Contrast** (Textbooks show how things are the same and how things are different.)

   The following is an example from an *English* textbook:

   Biographies and autobiographies are similar. They are both stories about a person's life. But autobiographies are stories that people write about their own lives, and biographies are stories people write about other people's lives.

   Your example from a _____ textbook:

   _____

   _____

   _____

   _____

   _____

2. **Time Order** (Textbooks tell things in the order that they happened or will happen.)

   The following is an example from a *cooking* textbook:

   To make a yeast mixture for baking bread, first put 3 cups of warm water in a bowl. Mix 3 packages of dry yeast into the water. Then, add 2 tablespoons of sugar. Cover the mixture for ten minutes with a towel. After about 5 minutes, the yeast mixture should start to bubble. If it bubbles, it is ready to be used.

   Your example from a _____ textbook:

   _____

   _____

   _____

   _____

   _____

The Writing Assignment *(cont.)*

3. **Cause and Effect** (Textbooks tell how or why something happened or will happen.)

    The following is an example from a *How to Bicycle* textbook:

    When you are on a bike, if you pedal forward, your bike will move forward. The faster you pedal forward, the faster your bike will move. There are a few ways to stop your bike. One way is to squeeze the hand brakes. Some bikes let you brake by pedaling backwards. You can also stop a bike by falling off of it, but that might hurt.

    Your example from a _____ textbook:

    _____

    _____

4. **Idea and Support** (Textbooks tell an idea, and then explain the idea.)

    The following is an example from a *How to Plan a Party* textbook.

    Before you throw a surprise party, make sure that it is the right kind of party for you to throw. Surprise parties are not right for everyone. Some people like to help plan their parties. That way, they can help make the guest list and the menu. Some people like to look forward to a party. It makes them feel happy. Some people just do not like surprises. Surprise parties can be fun, but make sure it is right for your party.

    Your example from a _____ textbook:

    _____

    _____

5. **Problem and Solution** (Textbooks tell a problem and then tell how to solve the problem, or how the problem was solved.)

    The following is an example from a *Helping Children Learn* textbook.

    All people get mad. Even best friends get mad at each other. Kids need to learn what they can do when they get mad. One good thing to do is to talk. Another good thing is to write a letter. Sometimes, it is best to walk away and do nothing.

    Your example from a _____ textbook:

    _____

    _____

The Reading Connection

Teacher Directions: Evaluate the charts.

Objective	Possible Points	Earned Points
You found and understand how to use different parts of a textbook.		
You made predictions about what might be in a textbook.		
You understand how textbooks are different from other books.		
Total Earned Points:		

The Writing Connection

Teacher Directions: Evaluate the paragraphs.

Objective	Possible Points	Earned Points
You wrote information in different ways: compare/contrast, problem/solution, time order, cause/effect, idea/support.		
You used words that were special to your topic.		
You put effort into spelling uncommon words correctly.		
You put effort into the writing process.		
Total Earned Points:		

Additional Teacher Comments: _____

_____

_____

Objectives

Reading

✔ To identify reasons people read at different speeds

Writing

✔ To write paragraphs describing personal reading habits

✔ To use topic sentences

✔ To identify and edit run-on sentences

Lesson Summary

The students will read an article called "The Speed of Reading." The students will identify when readers read carefully, skim, and/or skip content. Then students will write paragraphs that describe their own reading habits.

Materials Needed

✳ copies of the reading assignment (pages 113–114)

✳ copies of the writing assignment (pages 115–116)

Part I: The Reading Connection

A. Develop interest in the topic.

Open up a discussion with students about different speeds people use when they walk. *Ask the following types of questions:* "What is your favorite walking speed? When do you walk fast? When do you walk slowly? What speed do you use when walking in the mall? What speed do you use when walking in the hallways at school?"

B. Encourage students to make predictions about the reading.

Tell the students that they will be reading a story called "The Speed of Reading." *Ask:* "Based on the title of the article, what do you think this article might be about?" Allow students to give creative answers.

C. Encourage good reading habits.

Explain that readers need to read at different speeds at different times. Explain that "The Speed of Reading" will teach students how to decide when to . . .

✳ *skim* (i.e., to read quickly to get the main idea)

✳ *skip ahead* (i.e., move on to more important information)

✳ *read slowly and carefully.*

Part I: The Reading Connection *(cont.)*

D. Establish a purpose for reading.

Explain that "The Speed of Reading" is an informational article and that the students are reading it to learn information. Pass out copies of "The Speed of Reading" (page 113) for the students to read. Go over the chart (page 114) that they should complete during the reading.

E. Define and extend word meaning.

Ask students if they have ever skimmed a rock or seen anyone skimming rocks. Ask students what it means to skim. *Skim* means to touch the top of something. Ask students to predict what it might mean when readers skim. (*When readers skim, they look quickly over the words to get a general idea of what is written.*)

F. Allow ample time for students to read the story and complete the reading assignment.

Some students might have trouble reading the material by themselves. You might want to read "The Speed of Reading" aloud to the students, or you might wish to have the students complete this reading activity in small groups.

G. Discuss the answers to the reading assignment together.

Here is an example of how students might fill in the chart on page 114.

When you are reading for . . .	and . . .	At what speed should you read? Should you skim, skip, or read slowly?
fun	it is interesting	*read slowly*
fun	it is important	*read slowly*
fun	it is boring but important	*skim*
fun	it is boring and not important	*skip*
information	you are looking for the information you need	*skim*
information	you find the information	*read slowly*

How did you read this article, and why? Answers to this question will vary. Students might write that they read this article slowly and carefully because they were looking for information to fill out their charts. Students might have skimmed to find the answers, as well.

Part II: The Writing Connection

A. Develop interest in the topic.

1. Write three columns on the board. Label the columns **Slow, Skim,** and **Skip**.

2. Ask the students to list things that they read *slowly*. Write their responses on the board under the **Slow** column. Encourage answers such as descriptions of main characters or setting, dialogue, directions, definitions, information they need for classes, notes from friends, lists from parents, etc.

3. Ask the students to list things that they *skim*. (These will be things that they read for the main idea.) Write their responses on the board. Encourage answers such as new articles, textbooks to find information that they need, long descriptions in books, computer websites, etc.

4. Ask the students to list things that they *skip* as they read. (These will be things that are not important and not interesting to them.) Write their responses on the board. Encourage answers such as something they already know, something that is boring, etc.

B. Explain the writing assignment to the students.

Tell the students that they will be thinking about their own reading patterns and answering the following questions (page 115):

1. What types of things do you read slowly and carefully?

2. What types of things do you skim as you read?

3. When do you skip things as you read?

4. How can you be a better reader by changing the speed that you read different things?

Remind students that all readers change their speed of reading as they read. Explain that as readers, they should be aware that they need to read some things slowly, skim other things, and skip some things completely.

C. Assist students in organizing their answers.

Give students a copy of the chart on page 116. Using the ideas on the board and adding more of their own, students should fill out the chart so that the answers apply to their individual reading habits. Encourage students to really think about how they read.

D. Allow writing time.

Give students ample time to answer the questions in the form of paragraphs. As they are working, walk around the room offering guidance.

Part II: The Writing Connection *(cont.)*

E. Give students a strategy to help them revise their writing.

Explain that a good paragraph starts with a topic sentence. A topic sentence is a sentence that tells what information is going to be in the paragraph. Together with the students, discuss possible topic sentences for the paragraphs that they are writing. Answers will vary but could include the following:

1. *There are many different things that I read slowly and carefully.*
   I read certain things slowly and carefully.

2. *There are many different things that I skim as I read.*
   As I read, there are some things that I skim.

3. *There are many things that I skip as I read.*
   Sometimes I skip things as I read.

4. *There are some things that I can change so that I can become a better reader.*
   I am going to try some things differently so that I can be a stronger reader.

Give students time to revise, using the new skill.

F. Give students a strategy to help them edit their writing.

Remind students that as they edit, they should look for run-on sentences. Run-on sentences are sentences that have more than one sentence inside of them. Sentences that are too long become confusing to read. Show students this example of a run-on sentence:

I skim over my science book to find definitions I skim history books to find answers to questions.

Have students look in their paragraphs to try to find examples of run-on sentences. Have them share their run-on sentences aloud.

Then, show students two ways to edit the incorrect sentence:

1. One way is to split the sentence up into two sentences.
   I skim over my science book to find definitions. I skim history books to find answers to questions.

2. The other way is to add a comma and a connecting word.
   I skim over my science book to find definitions, and I skim history books to find answers to questions.

Give students time to edit their run-on sentences, using the new skill.

G. Publish students' ideas.

Have students exchange papers and select a part of a paragraph that they think is well written. Have them share the selection aloud, either in small groups or as a class.

The Reading Assignment

Directions: Read "The Speed of Reading" below and fill in the chart on page 114.

The Speed of Reading

People read at different speeds for different reasons.

* Sometimes, readers read very fast. This is called *skimming*. When a person skims, the reader is just getting the idea of what is written. The reader is not really reading every word.

* Sometimes, readers read so fast that they skip a full sentence or even more. This is called *skipping*.

* Sometimes, readers read so slowly that they read every word. This is called *reading very carefully*. When a reader reads very carefully, sometimes the reader even reads the same words more than once.

How do readers know how fast or slowly to read?

Sometimes when people read, it is not for fun. Sometimes, people read for information. When readers are reading for fun, they can pick how fast they want to read something.

* If something is interesting and important to the reader, the reader might want to read slowly.

* If something is boring to the reader, but is important, the reader should skim the words.

* If something is boring and not important, the reader should skip the words.

* Readers can skim to find the information that they need.

* Readers can skip over information that they do not need.

* Readers should slow down and read carefully when they find the information that they need.

Good readers know that reading speeds change. Sometimes readers read fast. Sometimes they read slowly. Sometimes, they choose not to read something. How did you read this article, and why?

The Reading Assignment *(cont.)*

As you read, fill in the chart and answer the question below.

When you are reading for . . .	and . . .	At what speed should you read? Should your skim, skip, or read slowly?
fun	it is interesting	
fun	it is important	
fun	it is boring but important	
fun	it is boring and not important	
information	you are looking for the information you need	
information	you find the information	

How did **you** read this article, and why?

_____

_____

_____

_____

The Writing Assignment

Directions: Write paragraphs explaining *how* you read. Then fill in the chart on page 116.

1. **What types of things do you read slowly and carefully?**

2. **What types of things do you skim as you read?**

3. **When do you skip things as you read?**

4. **How can you be a better reader by changing the speed that you read different things?**

The Writing Assignment *(cont.)*

I SLOWLY READ	I SKIM	I SKIP

The Reading Connection

Teacher Directions: Evaluate the answers to the reading assignment.

Objective	Possible Points	Earned Points
You understand when readers change the speed of their reading.		
Total Earned Points:		

The Writing Connection

Teacher Directions: Evaluate the answers to the writing assignment.

Objective	Possible Points	Earned Points
You described your reading habits.		
You found a way to try to improve as a reader.		
You used topic sentences.		
You avoided run-on sentences.		
You put effort into using the writing process effectively.		
Total Earned Points:		

Additional Teacher Comments: _____

_____

_____

_____

Lesson
Fourteen

Objectives

Reading

✔ To make and revise predictions while reading

Writing

✔ To write a prediction of your life in the future

✔ To use different words when starting sentences

✔ To separate ideas into paragraphs

Lesson Summary

The students will read "Think Again" (page 122–123) and make and revise predictions as they read the story. Then, the students will write a prediction of what their lives will be like in the future.

Materials Needed

✱ copies of the reading assignment (pages 122–123)

✱ copies of the writing assignment (page 124)

Part I: The Reading Connection

A. Develop interest in the topic.

Ask: "Did you ever guess that something was going to happen? For example, did you guess someone was planning a surprise for you? Did you guess what a present was going to be? Did you guess you were going to have a pop quiz? Did you guess you were going to dislike a movie?" Answers will vary. Encourage students to discuss their experiences.

B. Encourage students to make predictions about the reading.

1. Explain that we always make guesses about what is going to happen to us in our own lives. For example, when we go to bed late, we guess that we will be tired the next day. When we make plans, we are guessing that we can carry out the plans.

2. Teach students that good readers are always making guesses while they are reading, too. These guesses are called *predictions*. Readers think about what they are reading and make guesses about what will happen next based on their own experiences and the clues that are given in the story.

3. Tell the students that they will be reading a story called "Think Again." Ask students to make predictions about the story. *Ask:* "Based on the title of the story, what do you think this story might be about?" Allow students to give creative answers.

Part I: The Reading Connection *(cont.)*

C. Encourage good reading habits.

Ask students to think about their own reading habits. Have them think about whether or not they make predictions, or guesses, as they read.

Ask students to discuss what types of predictions readers can make. Answers will vary but should be similar to the following:

* ✳ What is going to happen next?
* ✳ What should a character do or say?
* ✳ What might happen if a character does or says something?
* ✳ What could have happened if a character did or said something differently?

Remind students that sometimes readers make predictions that are right and sometimes they make predictions that are wrong. Explain to the students that if they make a wrong prediction, that does not mean that they are bad readers. Good readers realize that sometimes predictions are right and sometimes predictions are wrong. Good readers constantly change their predictions as they get more information.

D. Establish a purpose for reading.

Pass out copies of "Think Again" (pages 122–123) for the students to read. Explain to the students that as they read the story, they will be asked to predict what might happen next. They should write their predictions in the space provided.

This story is divided into sections to encourage students to make predictions. After copying the story, cut it apart into the different sections and distribute each section only after the students have made their predictions.

E. Define and extend word meaning.

Remind the students that the word *prediction* means "guess." Write the word on the board. Break up the word for the students: pre/diction. Remind students that *pre-* is a common beginning of words, and it means "before." *Diction* means "word." A *prediction* is "saying something (using words) before it happens." You might want to point out that the root *dict* is in the word *dictionary*, a book of words.

F. Allow ample time for students to read the story and complete the reading assignment.

G. Discuss the answers to the reading assignment together.

Answers will vary. Allow students time to share predictions that they made that were correct and incorrect, but encourage students to justify why they made each prediction that they did.

Lesson Fourteen

Part II: The Writing Connection

A. Develop interest in the topic.

Have the students picture themselves five minutes from now, five hours from now, five days from now, five years from now, 15 years from now, and 50 years from now.

B. Explain the writing assignment to the students.

Tell the students that they will be making some predictions about their lives. Remind students that a prediction is a guess. Hand out page 124 to the students. Read the assignment aloud to them. "Make some predictions about your life in the future. Describe the time, the place, and what is happening to you in your life." Tell students that their predictions can take place five minutes from now, many years into the future, or anywhere in between.

C. Assist students in organizing their predictions.

Help the students gather their ideas. Read aloud the questions on their writing-assignment handout and allow them time to answer each question. Encourage some creative thinking by asking students additional questions such as the following:

1. How far into the future is your prediction?

 ✳ Is there something exciting that you are hoping will happen soon?

 ✳ Are you looking forward to a wonderful trip or activity?

 ✳ Is your family planning anything new?

 ✳ Are you planning to try something new?

 ✳ Do you know what you want to do when you grow up?

 ✳ Do you plan on attending college?

2. Where are you? What does it look like around you?

 ✳ Are you outside or inside?

 ✳ Are you in the similar time period as today, or are you in a future that looks different?

 ✳ Do you own your own place? What does it look like?

 ✳ Are you in a workplace? What does it look like?

3. What do you look like?

 ✳ What are you wearing?

 ✳ Are the styles the same as today or different?

 ✳ What does your hair look like?

Part II: The Writing Connection *(cont.)*

4. What is happening to you? What is your life like? What are you doing?

✽ How are you feeling? Are you happy or sad?

✽ Do you work?

✽ Do you have other responsibilities?

✽ Are you on vacation?

✽ Who are your family members?

D. Allow writing time.

Give students ample time to begin writing their predictions. As they are working, walk around the room and offer guidance.

E. Give students a strategy to help them revise their writing.

Have students check to see that they do not start each sentence with the same word (for instance, the word *I*). Share with the students other ways to start sentences, such as the following:

✽ In the future,   ✽ Inside

✽ Soon,   ✽ My home is

✽ Someday,   ✽ My hair is

✽ My family is   ✽ The clothes I am wearing are

✽ Outside,   ✽ Being a _____ is my job.

Give students time to revise their writing.

F. Give students a strategy to help them edit their writing.

Remind students that when starting a new idea, they might want to start a new paragraph, as well. For example, if students are writing about their home in the future in one paragraph, they might want to put the information about their future job in another paragraph.

Give students time to edit, using the new skill.

G. Publish students' ideas.

Option 1: Have students share parts of their future predictions with the rest of the class.

Option 2: Have students select a piece of their predictions for you to read, and have the rest of the class guess who wrote which prediction.

Lesson Fourteen

The Reading Assignment

Directions: Read "Think Again" and make predictions about how the story will continue.

Think Again

Moms always say goofy things. One goofy thing my mom always says is, "Don't forget to think." I guess I should have listened to her.

Make a prediction about what will happen next: _____

_____

_____

✄ —

It all started on a Monday morning. I woke up late as usual. I got ready for school, quickly. Then, I ran downstairs, tripping over a game I had played with a few days ago.

"Do you have everything you need for the day?" Mom asked me. "Sure," I answered without thinking.

Was your last prediction right? _____

Make a new prediction: _____

_____

_____

✄ —

I rushed out the door, slamming it behind me. I ran to the bus stop as the bus was just pulling away. It stopped for me. I got on the bus, and it started moving. It was then that I realized I had forgotten my lunch. The rest of the day did not go much better.

Was your last prediction right? _____

Make a new prediction: _____

_____

_____

The Reading Assignment *(cont.)*

Think Again

I had gotten in trouble in math class for forgetting my homework. My friend was mad at me for something I forgot to do. And I hurt my finger in cooking class because I didn't think to put on a mitten before taking a lid off of a hot pot.

After school, I decided to walk home because it was such a nice day. I didn't think to call my mom to tell her I'd be a little late.

Was your last prediction right? _____

Make a new prediction: _____

_____

_____

✂ –

When I finally got home, I was tired, hot, hungry, and a bit grumpy. And the front door was locked.

Was your last prediction right? _____

Make a new prediction: _____

_____

_____

✂ –

All I could do was sit on the front porch and wait. Suddenly, I heard a noise.

Was your last prediction right? _____

Make a new prediction: _____

_____

_____

✂ –

It sounded like a group of people singing "Happy Birthday." It was! I saw a bunch of my family and friends walking towards my house, singing together.

"We went to meet you at the bus stop," my mom said, "but you weren't there."

"I should have called. I'm sorry," I said. "I forgot today was my birthday."

"For once it is okay that you did not think," my mom said, "because we remembered!"

The Writing Assignment

Directions: Make a prediction about your life in the future. Describe the time, the place, and what is happening to you in your life.

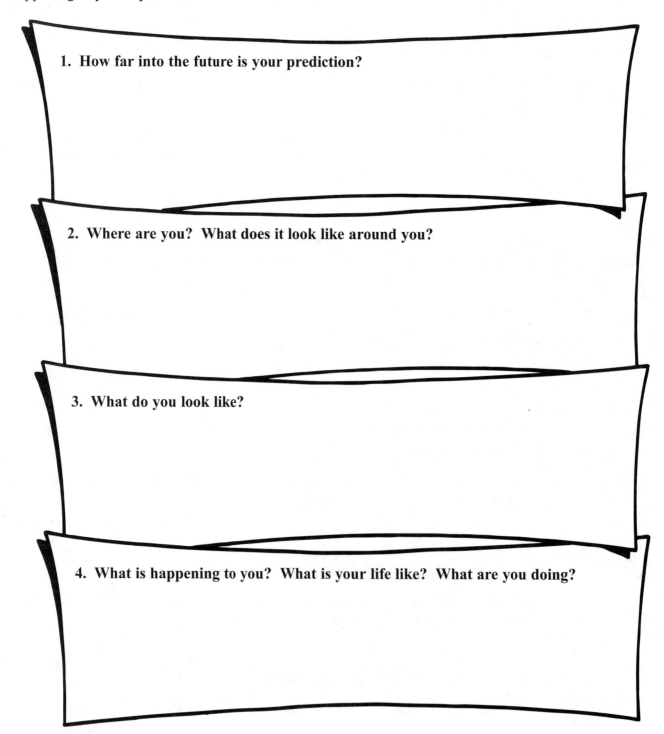

1. How far into the future is your prediction?

2. Where are you? What does it look like around you?

3. What do you look like?

4. What is happening to you? What is your life like? What are you doing?

The Reading Connection

Teacher Directions: Evaluate the answers on the reading handout.

Objective	Possible Points	Earned Points
You made predictions as you read.		
You knew whether your predictions were right or wrong.		
Total Earned Points:		

The Writing Connection

Teacher Directions: Evaluate the predictions.

Objective	Possible Points	Earned Points
You wrote a prediction of your life in the future.		
You started your sentences with different words.		
You put different ideas into different paragraphs.		
You put effort into the writing process.		
Total Earned Points:		

Additional Teacher Comments: _____

_____

_____

_____

_____

Objectives

Reading

- ✔ To identify the narrator of a story
- ✔ To find the beginning, middle, and end of a story
- ✔ To define and find examples of personification

Writing

- ✔ To write a narrative
- ✔ To select a point of view to tell a story
- ✔ To punctuate and use transitions correctly

Lesson Summary

The students will read a story called "Enjoy Today." Then, the students will write a narrative story. This narrative will be told by an object of the students' choice.

Materials Needed

- ✻ copies of the reading assignment (pages 129–130)
- ✻ copies of the writing assignment (page 131)
- ✻ picture of a pink magnolia tree in full bloom (*optional*)
- ✻ colored pencils, crayons, or markers (*optional*)

Part I: The Reading Connection

A. Develop interest in the topic.

Hold up a piece of chalk. *Ask:* "If this chalk could talk, what might it tell you about its day yesterday?" Answers will vary. Encourage creative responses.

B. Encourage students to make predictions about the reading.

1. Tell the students that they will be reading a story told by a magnolia flower. Some magnolia trees bloom with pink flowers in the springtime. The story is called "Enjoy Today." If you have a picture of a magnolia tree, you might want to show it to the students.

2. Ask students to make predictions about the story. *Ask:* "What do you think the magnolia flower will say in the story?" Allow students to give creative answers.

C. Encourage good reading habits.

Remind students that a narrator is the person who is telling the story. The narrator in this story is not a person, however: the narrator in this story is the flower.

Students should be aware that someone or something tells every story. As students read, they should look for the narrator.

Lesson
Fifteen

Part I: The Reading Connection *(cont.)*

D. Establish a purpose for reading.

Pass out copies of "Enjoy Today" (page 129) for the students to read. Read aloud the instructions that the students should complete as they read the story.

E. Define and extend word meaning.

The word *personified* is used in the instructions. Tell the students that when something that is not human acts like a human, that is called *personification*. When something is personified, that object is made to act like a human. For example, if an author wrote that the chalk danced around the board, that would be an example of personification.

Tell students that as they read, they should look for ways the author made the magnolia flower act like a human.

F. Allow ample time for students to read the story and complete the reading assignment.

G. Discuss the answers to the reading assignment together.

1.–3. Have students share the pictures that they drew. Have them explain why they chose to draw the image that they did.

4. Answers will vary. The author gave the flower a voice in the story. In that way, the author personified the flower. Other answer might include the following:

* I broke out of my shell . . .
* I stretched . . .
* I love . . .
* I reached, trying to touch the warm rays . . .
* I saw myself . . .

* I happily danced . . .
* I looked around . . .
* My sisters and cousins . . .
* I know that . . .

Part II: The Writing Connection

A. Develop interest in the topic.

Have students list objects that spend part of the day with them. Objects might include a pen, book bag, remote control, computer, toothbrush, shirt, glasses, cell phone, etc.

Part II: The Writing Connection *(cont.)*

B. Explain the writing assignment to the students.

Explain to the students that they will be writing a narrative. A *narrative* is a story with a beginning, a middle, and an end. This narrative will be a true event that happened to them, but the students will not be telling the story. The students will need to select an object to tell the story! Read aloud the following example of a toothbrush telling a story:

> *Every morning I hear beeping in the other room. Sometimes the sun is up, and other times the sun is not up yet. Soon, my friend Anna comes into my room and picks me up. She puts this blue, minty goop on me, and then puts me in her mouth. Suddenly, I am being tickled all over. I can barley stand it! About a minute goes by, and then Anna puts me in some water. That feels good after being tickled for so long! Soon, she puts me down, and I can go back to sleep until the evening. "Have a good day," I whisper as Anna leaves the room, "and smile a lot!"*

In this example, the toothbrush is telling the story the way it sees things happening. That is called *point of view*. Point of view is the way the storyteller sees the story.

C. Assist students in organizing their narrative.

Hand out page 131. Help the students gather their ideas. Read aloud the questions on their writing-assignment handout and allow students time to answer each question. Have the students share some of their ideas with the rest of the class.

D. Allow writing time.

Give students ample time to write their narratives.

E. Give students a strategy to help them revise their writing.

Tell students that when writing a narrative, there are some words that can be used to help move the story along from beginning to end. These words are called transitions. Some useful transitions for a narrative might be *to begin, then, soon, after that, suddenly, finally,* and *in the end.*

Give students time to revise their work.

F. Give students a strategy to help them edit their writing.

Tell students that after a transition is used, students should place a comma (e.g., "Soon, my friend Anna will come into my room and pick me up.")

Give students time to edit, using the new skill.

G. Publish students' ideas.

Have students take turns passing around each other's papers and reading different narratives.

The Reading Assignment

Directions: Read "Enjoy Today" and follow the instructions on page 130.

Enjoy Today

All winter long, I was nowhere to be seen. But once the weather warmed and the rain began to fall and the sun shone and the ground became warm, I began to grow.

I started off looking like a little brown point sticking out of a tree branch. Then, I grew bigger. Soon, I looked like a greenish, fuzzy, oval-shaped shell. It was not long before I broke out of my fuzzy oval shell.

I stretched and stretched. I loved the warmth of the sun. I reached up, trying to touch the warm rays of the sun.

It was then that I saw myself in the reflection of a window pane. Wow, was I beautiful! My center was dark pink, and the tips of my petals were a lighter pink. I happily danced in the light breeze.

I looked all around. My sisters and cousins were just as happy as I was, and they were looking just as beautiful.

Birds landed near us and sang us songs. Squirrels smelled our sweet scent. People would point and say, "Wow, look at that magnolia tree."

I know that my beauty will not last forever, but I will enjoy today.

The Reading Assignment *(cont.)*

Directions: As you read "Enjoy Today," do the following:

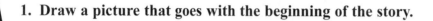

1. Draw a picture that goes with the beginning of the story.

2. Draw a picture that goes with the middle of the story.

3. Draw a picture that goes with the end of the story.

4. How is the flower personified in the story?

Lesson Fifteen

The Writing Assignment

Directions: Write a story with a beginning, middle, and end. The story should be true and should have happened to you. (*It can be an event that happens all of the time or something unusual that happened.*) Have an object tell the story!

What object will tell your story? _____

What happens at the beginning of your story?

_____

_____

_____

_____

What happens in the middle of your story?

_____

_____

_____

_____

How does your story end?

_____

_____

_____

_____

Lesson
Fifteen

The Reading Connection

Teacher Directions: Evaluate the answers on the reading handout.

Objective	Possible Points	Earned Points
You found the beginning, middle, and end of the story.		
You show how the flower was personified in the story.		
Total Earned Points:		

The Writing Connection

Teacher Directions: Evaluate the narrative stories.

Objective	Possible Points	Earned Points
You wrote a story with a beginning, middle, and end.		
You wrote a story using a specific point of view.		
You punctuated and used transitions in your writing.		
Total Earned Points:		

Additional Teacher Comments: _____

_____

_____

_____

_____

_____

National Standard Correlations

Listed below are the McREL standards for Language Arts Level 2 (Grades 3–5). All standards and benchmarks are used with permission from McREL.

Copyright 2004 McREL

Mid-continent Research for Education and Learning

2550 S. Parker Road, Suite 500

Aurora, CO 80014

Telephone: (303) 337-0990

Website: *www.mcrel.org/standards-benchmarks*

McREL Standards are in **bold**. Benchmarks are in regular print. The correlating lessons that meet each objective are in *italics*.

Standard 1: Uses the general skills and strategies of the writing process.

1. Prewriting: Uses prewriting strategies to plan written work (e.g., uses graphic organizers, story maps, and webs; groups related ideas; takes notes; brainstorms ideas; organizes information according to type and purpose of writing)

   ◆ *Lesson One*   ◆ *Lesson Six*   ◆ *Lesson Ten*

   ◆ *Lesson Two*   ◆ *Lesson Seven*   ◆ *Lesson Thirteen*

   ◆ *Lesson Three*   ◆ *Lesson Eight*   ◆ *Lesson Fourteen*

   ◆ *Lesson Four*   ◆ *Lesson Nine*   ◆ *Lesson Fifteen*

   ◆ *Lesson Five*

2. Drafting and Revising: Uses strategies to draft and revise written work (e.g., elaborates on a central idea; writes with attention to audience, word choice, sentence variation; uses paragraphs to develop separate ideas; produces multiple drafts)

   ◆ *Lesson One*   ◆ *Lesson Six*   ◆ *Lesson Eleven*

   ◆ *Lesson Two*   ◆ *Lesson Seven*   ◆ *Lesson Twelve*

   ◆ *Lesson Three*   ◆ *Lesson Eight*   ◆ *Lesson Fourteen*

   ◆ *Lesson Four*   ◆ *Lesson Ten*   ◆ *Lesson Fifteen*

   ◆ *Lesson Five*

Standard 1 *(cont.)*

3. Editing and Publishing: Uses strategies to edit and publish written work (e.g., edits for grammar, punctuation, capitalization, and spelling at a developmentally appropriate level; uses reference materials; considers page format [paragraphs, margins, indentations, titles]; selects presentation format according to purpose; incorporates photos, illustrations, charts, and graphs; uses available technology to compose and publish work)

✦ *Lesson One*	✦ *Lesson Six*	✦ *Lesson Eleven*
✦ *Lesson Two*	✦ *Lesson Seven*	✦ *Lesson Twelve*
✦ *Lesson Three*	✦ *Lesson Eight*	✦ *Lesson Thirteen*
✦ *Lesson Four*	✦ *Lesson Nine*	✦ *Lesson Fourteen*
✦ *Lesson Five*	✦ *Lesson Ten*	✦ *Lesson Fifteen*

4. Evaluates own and others' writing (e.g., determines the best features of a piece of writing, determines how own writing achieves its purposes, asks for feedback, responds to classmates' writing)

✦ *Lesson Two*	✦ *Lesson Eight*	✦ *Lesson Eleven*
✦ *Lesson Three*	✦ *Lesson Ten*	✦ *Lesson Thirteen*

5. Uses strategies (e.g., adapts focus, organization, point of view; determines knowledge and interests of audience) to write for different audiences (e.g., self, peers, teachers, adults)

   ✦ *Lesson Eight*

6. Uses strategies (e.g., adapts focus, point of view, organization, form) to write for a variety of purposes (e.g., to inform, entertain, explain, describe, record ideas)

✦ *Lesson Three*	✦ *Lesson Eight*	✦ *Lesson Twelve*
✦ *Lesson Five*	✦ *Lesson Nine*	✦ *Lesson Fifteen*
✦ *Lesson Six*	✦ *Lesson Ten*	

7. Writes expository compositions (e.g., identifies and stays on the topic; develops the topic with simple facts, details, examples, and explanations; excludes extraneous and inappropriate information; uses structures such as cause-and-effect, chronology, similarities and differences; uses several sources of information; provides a concluding statement)

✦ *Lesson One*	✦ *Lesson Six*	✦ *Lesson Twelve*
✦ *Lesson Five*	✦ *Lesson Eight*	

Standard 1 *(cont.)*

8. Writes narrative accounts, such as poems and stories (e.g., establishes a context that enables the reader to imagine the event or experience; develops characters, setting, and plot; creates an organizing structure; sequences events; uses concrete sensory details; uses strategies such as dialogue, tension, and suspense; uses an identifiable voice)

   - ✦ *Lesson Three*
   - ✦ *Lesson Four*
   - ✦ *Lesson Seven*
   - ✦ *Lesson Ten*
   - ✦ *Lesson Eleven*
   - ✦ *Lesson Fifteen*

9. Writes autobiographical compositions (e.g., provides a context within which the incident occurs, uses simple narrative strategies, and provides some insight into why this incident is memorable)

   - ✦ *Lesson Seven*
   - ✦ *Lesson Fifteen*

10. Writes expressive compositions (e.g., expresses ideas, reflections, and observations; uses an individual, authentic voice; uses narrative strategies, relevant details, and ideas that enable the reader to imagine the world of the event or experience)

    - ✦ *Lesson Two*
    - ✦ *Lesson Four*
    - ✦ *Lesson Nine*
    - ✦ *Lesson Thirteen*
    - ✦ *Lesson Fourteen*

11. Writes in response to literature (e.g., summarizes main ideas and significant details; relates own ideas to supporting details; advances judgments; supports judgments with references to the text, other works, other authors, nonprint media, and personal knowledge)

    - ✦ *Lesson Seven*
    - ✦ *Lesson Ten*

12. Writes personal letters (e.g., includes the date, address, greeting, body, and closing; addresses envelopes; includes signature)

    - ✦ *Lesson Six*
    - ✦ *Lesson Eight*

Standard 2: Uses the stylistic and rhetorical aspects of writing

1. Uses descriptive language that clarifies and enhances ideas (e.g., common figures of speech, sensory details)

   - ✦ *Lesson Two*
   - ✦ *Lesson Three*
   - ✦ *Lesson Nine*
   - ✦ *Lesson Ten*

National Standard Correlations *(cont.)*

Standard 2 *(cont.)*

2. Uses paragraph form in writing (e.g., indents the first word of a paragraph, uses topic sentences, recognizes a paragraph as a group of sentences about one main idea, uses an introductory and concluding paragraph, writes several related paragraphs)

   ✦ *Lesson One*   ✦ *Lesson Six*   ✦ *Lesson Thirteen*

   ✦ *Lesson Five*   ✦ *Lesson Seven*   ✦ *Lesson Fourteen*

3. Uses a variety of sentence structures in writing (e.g., expands basic sentence patterns, uses exclamatory and imperative sentences)

   ✦ *Lesson Four*   ✦ *Lesson Ten*   ✦ *Lesson Fourteen*

Standard 3: Uses grammatical and mechanical conventions in written compositions

1. Writes in cursive

2. Uses pronouns in written compositions (e.g., substitutes pronouns for nouns, uses pronoun agreement)

   ✦ *Lesson One*

3. Uses nouns in written compositions (e.g., uses plural and singular naming words, forms regular and irregular plurals of nouns, uses common and proper nouns, uses nouns as subjects)

4. Uses verbs in written compositions (e.g., uses a wide variety of action verbs, past and present verb tenses, simple tenses, forms of regular verbs, verbs that agree with the subject)

5. Uses adjectives in written compositions (e.g., indefinite, numerical, predicate adjectives)

   ✦ *Lesson Three*

6. Uses adverbs in written compositions (e.g., to make comparisons)

   ✦ *Lesson Three*

7. Uses coordinating conjunctions in written compositions (e.g., links ideas using connecting words)

   ✦ *Lesson Seven*   ✦ *Lesson Thirteen*   ✦ *Lesson Fifteen*

8. Uses negatives in written compositions (e.g., avoids double negatives)

Standard 3 *(cont.)*

9. Uses conventions of spelling in written compositions (e.g., spells high-frequency, commonly misspelled words from appropriate grade-level list; uses a dictionary and other resources to spell words; uses initial consonant substitution to spell related words; uses vowel combinations for correct spelling; uses contractions, compounds, roots, suffixes, prefixes, and syllable constructions to spell words)

10. Uses conventions of capitalization in written compositions (e.g., titles of people; proper nouns [names of towns, cities, counties, and states; days of the week; months of the year; names of streets; names of countries; holidays]; first word of direct quotations; heading, salutation, and closing of a letter)

   ✦ *Lesson Four* ✦ *Lesson Six* ✦ *Lesson Eleven*

11. Uses conventions of punctuation in written compositions (e.g., uses periods after imperative sentences and in initials, abbreviations, and titles before names; uses commas in dates and addresses and after greetings and closings in a letter; uses apostrophes in contractions and possessive nouns; uses quotation marks around titles and with direct quotations; uses a colon between hour and minutes)

   ✦ *Lesson Three* ✦ *Lesson Five* ✦ *Lesson Eight*

   ✦ *Lesson Four* ✦ *Lesson Six* ✦ *Lesson Ten*

Standard 4: Gathers and uses information for research purposes

1. Uses a variety of strategies to plan research (e.g., identifies possible topic by brainstorming, listing questions, using idea webs; organizes prior knowledge about a topic; develops a course of action; determines how to locate necessary information)

   ✦ *Lesson Five*

2. Uses encyclopedias to gather information for research topics

3. Uses dictionaries to gather information for research topics

4. Uses electronic media to gather information (e.g., databases, Internet, CD-ROM, television shows, cassette recordings, videos, pull-down menus, word searches)

5. Uses key words, guide words, alphabetical and numerical order, indexes, cross-references, and letters on volumes to find information for research topics

6. Uses multiple representations of information (e.g., maps, charts, photos, diagrams, tables) to find information for research topics

National Standard Correlations *(cont.)*

Standard 4 *(cont.)*

7. Uses strategies to gather and record information for research topics (e.g., uses notes, maps, charts, graphs, tables, and other graphic organizers; paraphrases and summarizes information; gathers direct quotes; provides narrative descriptions)

   ✦ *Lesson Five*

8. Uses strategies to compile information into written reports or summaries (e.g., incorporates notes into a finished product; includes simple facts, details, explanations, and examples; draws conclusions from relationships and patterns that emerge from data from different sources; uses appropriate visual aids and media)

   ✦ *Lesson One*   ✦ *Lesson Five*

9. Cites information sources (e.g., quotes or paraphrases information sources, lists resources used by title)

   ✦ *Lesson Five*

Standard 5: Uses the general skills and strategies of the reading process

1. Previews text (e.g., skims material; uses pictures, textual clues, and text format)

   ✦ *Lesson Five*

2. Establishes a purpose for reading (e.g., for information, for pleasure, to understand a specific viewpoint)

   ✦ *Lesson One*   ✦ *Lesson Five*   ✦ *Lesson Six*

3. Makes, confirms, and revises simple predictions about what will be found in a text (e.g., uses prior knowledge and ideas presented in text, illustrations, titles, topic sentences, key words, and foreshadowing clues)

✦ *Lesson One*	✦ *Lesson Six*	✦ *Lesson Eleven*
✦ *Lesson Two*	✦ *Lesson Seven*	✦ *Lesson Twelve*
✦ *Lesson Three*	✦ *Lesson Eight*	✦ *Lesson Thirteen*
✦ *Lesson Four*	✦ *Lesson Nine*	✦ *Lesson Fourteen*
✦ *Lesson Five*	✦ *Lesson Ten*	

Standard 5 *(cont.)*

4. Uses phonetic and structural analysis techniques, syntactic structure, and semantic context to decode unknown words (e.g., vowel patterns, complex word families, syllabication, root words, affixes)

   ✦ *Lesson One*   ✦ *Lesson Eight*   ✦ *Lesson Thirteen*

   ✦ *Lesson Two*   ✦ *Lesson Nine*   ✦ *Lesson Fourteen*

   ✦ *Lesson Four*   ✦ *Lesson Ten*

5. Uses a variety of context clues to decode unknown words (e.g., draws on earlier reading, reads ahead)

6. Uses word reference materials (e.g., glossary, dictionary, thesaurus) to determine the meaning, pronunciation, and derivations of unknown words

7. Understands level-appropriate reading vocabulary (e.g., synonyms, antonyms, homophones, multi-meaning words)

8. Monitors own reading strategies and makes modifications as needed (e.g., recognizes when he or she is confused by a section of text, questions whether the text makes sense)

9. Adjusts speed of reading to suit purpose and difficulty of the material

   ✦ *Lesson Ten*   ✦ *Lesson Thirteen*

10. Understands the author's purpose (e.g., to persuade, to inform) or point of view

    ✦ *Lesson Six*

11. Uses personal criteria to select reading material (e.g., personal interest, knowledge of authors and genres, text difficulty, recommendations of others)

Standard 6: Uses reading skills and strategies to understand and interpret a variety of literary texts

1. Uses reading skills and strategies to understand a variety of literary passages and texts (e.g., fairy tales, folktales, fiction, nonfiction, myths, poems, fables, fantasies, historical fiction, biographies, autobiographies, chapter books)

   ✦ *Lesson One*   ✦ *Lesson Three*   ✦ *Lesson Eleven*

   ✦ *Lesson Two*   ✦ *Lesson Four*

Standard 6 *(cont.)*

2. Knows the defining characteristics of a variety of literary forms and genres (e.g., fairy tales, folk tales, fiction, nonfiction, myths, poems, fables, fantasies, historical fiction, biographies, autobiographies, chapter books)

   ✦ *Lesson Two*   ✦ *Lesson Four*   ✦ *Lesson Five*

   ✦ *Lesson Three*

3. Understands the basic concept of plot (e.g., main problem, conflict, resolution, cause-and-effect)

   ✦ *Lesson Three*   ✦ *Lesson Eight*   ✦ *Lesson Eleven*

4. Understands similarities and differences within and among literary works from various genre and cultures (e.g., in terms of settings, character types, events, point of view; role of natural phenomena)

   ✦ *Lesson Ten*

5. Understands elements of character development in literary works (e.g., differences between main and minor characters; stereotypical characters as opposed to fully-developed characters; changes that characters undergo; the importance of a character's actions, motives, and appearance to plot and theme)

   ✦ *Lesson Ten*

6. Knows themes that recur across literary works

7. Understands the ways in which language is used in literary texts (e.g., personification, alliteration, onomatopoeia, simile, metaphor, imagery, hyperbole, beat, rhythm)

   ✦ *Lesson Nine*

8. Makes connections between characters or simple events in a literary work and people or events in his or her own life

   ✦ *Lesson Three*   ✦ *Lesson Seven*   ✦ *Lesson Ten*

Standard 7: Uses reading skills and strategies to understand and interpret a variety of informational texts

1. Uses reading skills and strategies to understand a variety of informational texts (e.g., textbooks, biographical sketches, letters, diaries, directions, procedures, magazines)

   ✦ *Lesson One*   ✦ *Lesson Twelve*   ✦ *Lesson Thirteen*

Standard 7 *(cont.)*

2. Knows the defining characteristics of a variety of informational texts (e.g., textbooks, biographical sketches, letters, diaries, directions, procedures, magazines)

   ✦ *Lesson One*   ✦ *Lesson Twelve*

3. Uses text organizers (e.g., headings, topic and summary sentences, graphic features, typeface, chapter titles) to determine the main ideas and to locate information in a text

   ✦ *Lesson Five*   ✦ *Lesson Twelve*

4. Uses the various parts of a book (e.g., index, table of contents, glossary, appendix, preface) to locate information

   ✦ *Lesson Twelve*

5. Summarizes and paraphrases information in texts (e.g., includes the main idea and significant supporting details of a reading selection)

   ✦ *Lesson Five*   ✦ *Lesson Eight*   ✦ *Lesson Ten*

6. Uses prior knowledge and experience to understand and respond to new information

   ✦ *Lesson Ten*   ✦ *Lesson Twelve*

7. Understands structural patterns or organization in informational texts (e.g., chronological, logical, or sequential order; compare-and-contrast; cause-and-effect; proposition and support)

   ✦ *Lesson Eight*

Standard 8: Uses listening and speaking strategies for different purposes

1. Contributes to group discussions

   ✦ *Lesson Three*   ✦ *Lesson Ten*

2. Asks questions in class (e.g., when he or she is confused, to seek others' opinions and comments)

3. Responds to questions and comments (e.g., gives reasons in support of opinions, responds to others' ideas)

4. Listens to classmates and adults (e.g., does not interrupt, faces the speaker, asks questions, summarizes or paraphrases to confirm understanding, gives feedback, eliminates barriers to effective listening)

   ✦ *Lesson Eight*

Standard 8 *(cont.)*

5. Uses strategies to convey a clear main point when speaking (e.g., expresses ideas in a logical manner, uses specific vocabulary to establish tone and present information)

6. Uses level-appropriate vocabulary in speech (e.g., familiar idioms, similes, word play)

   ✦ *Lesson Eight*

7. Makes basic oral presentations to class (e.g., uses subject-related information and vocabulary; includes content appropriate to the audience; relates ideas and observations; incorporates visual aids or props; incorporates several sources of information)

8. Uses a variety of nonverbal communication skills (e.g., eye contact, gestures, facial expressions, posture)

9. Uses a variety of verbal communication skills (e.g., projection, tone, volume, rate, articulation, pace, phrasing)

   ✦ *Lesson Eight*

10. Organizes ideas for oral presentations (e.g., uses an introduction and conclusion; uses notes or other memory aids; organizes ideas around major points, in sequence, or chronologically; uses traditional structures, such as cause-and-effect, similarity and difference, posing and answering a question; uses details, examples, and anecdotes to clarify information)

    ✦ *Lesson Eight*

11. Listens for specific information in spoken texts (e.g., plot details or information about a character in a short story read aloud, information about a familiar topic from a radio broadcast)

12. Understands the main ideas and supporting details in spoken texts (e.g., presentations by peers or quest speakers, a current affairs report on the radio)

13. Listens to and understands persuasive messages (e.g., television commercials, commands and requests, pressure from peers)

    ✦ *Lesson Six*

14. Interprets the use of nonverbal cues used in conversation

15. Knows specific ways in which language is used in real-life situations (e.g., buying something from a shopkeeper, requesting something from a parent, arguing with a sibling, talking to a friend)

    ✦ *Lesson Six*   ✦ *Lesson Eight*

16. Understands that language reflects different regions and cultures (e.g., sayings; expressions; usage; oral traditions and customs; historical, geographical, and societal influences on language)

References

Lesson One: Biographies

Bellis, Mary. "Scotch Tape and Richard Drew." About, Inc. A Primedia Company. 2004. (5 Feb. 2005.)

http://inventors.about.com/library/inventors/blscotchtape.htm

"Wilson A. Bentley." Jericho Historical Society. 2000. (4 Feb. 2005)

http://snowflakebentley.com>

Lesson Two: Fairy Tales

"Fairy Tales from Life." IRA/NCTE. Feb. 9, 2005. (10 Feb. 2005)

http://www.readwritethink.org/lessons/lesson_view.asp?id=42

Lesson Three: Fables

"Fable." Turner Learning, Inc. 1999. (8 Feb. 2005)

http://www.turnerlearning.com/tntlearning/animalfarm/affable.html

Cook, Kathy. "Elements of Fables." ArtsEdge and the John F. Kennedy Center for the Performing Arts. (7 Feb. 2005)

http://artsedge.kennedy-center.org/content/2221/

"Look Who's Talking." Nature Home. The Educational Broadcasting Corporation. 1997–2005. PBS Online. (8 Feb. 2005)

http://www.pbs.org/wnet/nature/parrots/html/intro.html

"Basic Rules for Using Commas." Factory School Community Handbook. October 2003. (6 Feb. 2005)

http://www.factoryschool.org/handbook/sentences/CommaRules.html

Lesson Four: Myths

Cook, Kathy. "Elements of Myths." ArtsEdge and the John F. Kennedy Center for the Performing Arts. (9 Feb. 2005)

http://artsedge.kennedy-center.org/content/2232/

Park, James and Corbett, Sally. "An Introduction to Ancient Greece: Greek and Roman Goddesses and Gods." Highland Park Elementary School. 1997. (9 Feb. 2005)

http://www.hipark.austin.isd.tenet.edu/mythology/gkgods_heroes.html

"African Gods and Their Associates." Untangle Incorporated. June 26, 2002. (9 Feb. 2005)

http://www.mythome.org/africang.html

"Names of Gods and Goddesses." Chinaroad. May 2003. (9 Feb. 2005)

http://www.lowchensaustralia.com/names/gods.htm

Lesson Five: Researching Folktales

"Create an MLA Works Cited Page." The Writing Center: University of Wisconsin-Madison. 2004. (18 Feb. 2005)

http://www.wisc.edu/writing/Handbook/DocMLA.html

Lamb, Annette and Johnson, Larry. "The topic: Tall Tales." 42eXplore: Thematic Pathfinders for all ages. Eduscape.com. April 2004. (14 Feb. 2005)

http://www.42explore.com/talltale.htm

Liukkonen, Petri. "Washington Irving." Books and Writers. 2000. (15 Feb 2005)

http://www.kirjasto.sci.fi/wirving.htm

Lesson Six: Persuasive Writing

"Format for a Friendly or Personal Letter." English Plus. 1997–2001. (19 Feb. 2005)

http://englishplus.com/grammar/00000144.htm

Lesson Nine: Literary Language

Ware, Robert. *OneLook Dictionary Search.* "Poetry." 1996. (6 March 2005)

http://www.onelook.com/

Lesson Fourteen: Making Predictions

Harper, Douglas. *Online Etymology Dictionary.* "Prediction." 2001. (4 April 2005)

http://www.etymonline.com/index.php?search=prediction&searchmode=none

National Standard Correlations

McREL: Mid-Continent Research for Education and Learning. "Content Knowledge—4th Edition." 2004. (14 Feb. 2005)

http://www.mcrel.org/compendium/browse.asp